...nary Activities

Cambridge Handbooks for Language Teachers

This is a series of practical guides for teachers of English and other languages. Illustrative examples are usually drawn from the field of English as a foreign or second language, but the ideas and techniques described can equally well be used in the teaching of any language.

Recent titles in this series:

Dictionary Activities

Cindy Leaney

CAMBRIDGE
UNIVERSITY PRESS

CAMBRIDGE UNIVERSITY PRESS
Cambridge, New York, Melbourne, Madrid, Cape Town, Singapore, São Paulo

Cambridge University Press
The Edinburgh Building, Cambridge CB2 8RU, UK

www.cambridge.org
Information on this title:
www.cambridge.org/9780521690409

© Cambridge University Press 2007

It is normally necessary for written permission for copying to be obtained *in advance* from a publisher. Certain parts of this book are designed to be copied and distributed in class. The normal requirements are waived here and it is not necessary to write to Cambridge University Press for permission for an individual teacher to make copies for use within his or her own classroom. Only those pages which carry the wording © Cambridge University Press 2007 may be copied.

First published 2007

Printed in the United Kingdom at the University Press, Cambridge

A catalogue record for this publication is available from the British Library

Library of Congress Cataloging-in-Publication Data
Leaney, Cindy.
   Dictionary activities / Cindy Leaney.
      p. cm. – (Cambridge handbooks for language teachers)
   Includes bibliographical references and index.
   ISBN 978-0-521-69040-9 (pbk.)
   1. English language–Dictionaries–Study and teaching. 2.
Vocabulary–Study and teaching. I. Title. II. Series.
   PE1611.L43 2007
   427.0071–dc22   2007002687

ISBN 978-0-521-69040-9 paperback

Cambridge University Press has no responsibility for the persistence or accuracy of URLs for external or third-party Internet websites referred to in this publication, and does not guarantee that any content on such websites is, or will remain, accurate or appropriate.

Contents

Thanks and acknowledgements

Author acknowledgements
My thanks to Pam Gadsby, Phil Scofield and Scott Thornbury for ideas and inspiration. Thanks to Frances Amrani and Alison Silver for attentive editing. Thanks also to Bob Harris for great music to write along to. Thanks to all the students over the years who have been so much fun. (And a big thank you to those students who have helped carry armfuls of dictionaries!) And special thanks to Tony Leaney for proofreading, reality checks and lunch.

Development of this publication has made use of the Cambridge International Corpus (CIC). The CIC is a computerized database of contemporary spoken and written English which currently stands at over one billion words. It includes British English, American English and other varieties of English. It also includes the Cambridge Learner Corpus, developed in collaboration with the University of Cambridge ESOL Examinations. Cambridge University Press has built up the CIC to provide evidence about language use that helps to produce better language teaching materials.

The author and publishers are grateful to the following for permission to reproduce copyright material. It has not been possible to identify the sources of all the material used and in such cases the publishers would welcome information from copyright owners.

pp. 47, 49, 55, 69, 109, 121, 123, 124 dictionary entries from *Cambridge Advanced Learner's Dictionary*, edited by P. Gillard, published by Cambridge University Press; pp. 6–7, 61, 68 dictionary entries from *Cambridge Learner's Dictionary*, edited by P. Gillard and E. Walter, published by Cambridge University Press; p. 92 text from 'The scientist that history forgot' by David Bodanis, *The Guardian*, 15 May 2006, p. 93 text from 'Deep in permafrost – a seed bank to save the world' by Alok Jha, *The Guardian*, 20 June 2006, and p. 103 adapted article 'Cheap anti-allergy drug offers hope of cure for malaria', by James Randerson, *The Guardian*, 3 July 2006 © Guardian Newspapers Ltd; p. 126 adapted article from

Dictionary Activities

Introduction

Learner dictionaries get better and better. They have more information and are easier to access and to understand than ever before. And, with the advent of electronic formats, space is no longer the problem it was.

There is a tremendous amount of information in a good learner's dictionary – sometimes an overwhelming amount. Helping students tap into that information efficiently is one of the best ways to help them become independent, lifelong language learners.

These activities are designed to foster good dictionary skills, help create good language learning habits and appeal to a variety of learning styles.

The activities are teacher-friendly and require little in the way of preparation or technology (apart from those that use the CD-ROM and some online activities) and can be adapted to a variety of language teaching contexts.

What makes learner dictionaries special?

The activities are based on the features of learner dictionaries that have become standard: clear definitions written using a graded defining vocabulary, frequency indicators, collocation information, navigational devices, example sentences, pronunciation, grammar and usage information.

When **choosing a dictionary**, it is worth taking the time to decide which features are most important to you and your students, and to evaluate how well designed the features are in each dictionary.

Defining vocabularies
One of the most distinctive differences between dictionaries written for native speakers of a language and learners of that language is that the definitions in learner dictionaries are written using a restricted defining vocabulary.

The number of words, or more accurately the number of senses of words, in a defining vocabulary varies, depending on the level of the dictionary.

An advanced level dictionary normally uses around 2,000 words in its defining vocabulary, an intermediate about 1,600 and a basic dictionary about 1,200.

Inclusion criteria

One of the first steps in creating a dictionary is deciding which words to define. Now that dictionary makers have access to huge databases of language, called *corpora*, they are able to make very informed decisions about a word's frequency in different contexts (spoken v. written, academic, business, etc.), the word's coverage and range, and the words it frequently co-occurs with (its collocations).

Navigational devices

All the major learner dictionaries have navigational devices to help the user find the right sense of a word. They are called guidewords, signposts, menus or shortcuts.

The first chapter in this book has activities to practise using these devices and to help build dictionary confidence.

Example sentences

Example or model sentences are usually taken from written or spoken corpora. They may be modified to make them more accessible. Whereas advanced dictionaries opt for full sentences, on the whole, the tendency in intermediate dictionaries is to include only sentence fragments in entries for all but the most frequent words. This is simply due to lack of space – intermediate dictionary formats are smaller.

However, dictionaries on CD-ROM can hold more text and so may have an examples bank. It depends on how much space is used for sound, video, interactive exercises, etc.

Style and usage labels

These labels tell the user when, where and how words and phrases are used. They may indicate whether a word is marked as formal or informal, whether it is used in different ways in certain contexts, and whether it is specific to a variety of English (e.g. British, American or Australian).

Multi-word items and collocations

Vocabulary teaching has recognized how important it is to teach (and learn!) chunks of language, rather than individual words. Chunks include formulaic expressions (*Have a nice day!*), sayings and catchphrases (*better late than never, make my day*); many idioms (*a red herring, down in the dumps*); phrasal verbs (*to get on with, to run out of*), many discourse markers (*by the way, as a matter of fact*), and fixed or semi-fixed collocations (*wishful thinking, behind bars*). The best of the dictionaries present this information clearly and efficiently.

Some things to consider when choosing a dictionary

What navigational devices are there? Are they easy to use?

How many headwords are there? Are inclusion criteria described?

Are definitions clear? Is there a defining vocabulary? How many words does it consist of? Is it listed at the back of the book?

Are example sentences useful?

Are there good style and usage labels?

How is pronunciation represented?

Are the grammar and usage notes clear?

Is it easy to find multi-word items (phrasal verbs, idioms)?

Are collocations included?

Are there study pages, and are these useful?

Is there any website support (worksheets, lesson plans, etc.) for the teacher?

Are there student resources (interactive activities online, links, etc.) on the website?

The activities

This book is designed so that teachers can 'dip in' and select the activities that are most suitable for your students and your teaching context, and those that will be most helpful in meeting your teaching objectives.

The activities are grouped into chapters. There is a short introduction at the beginning of each chapter to help you find the activities you want to use.

Have a look at the Contents on pages v–viii, decide which chapter best suits your lesson focus, read the short introduction, then flick through the activity titles in that chapter.

Each activity is laid out to show the aim, focus, level and time plus any preparation needed. Then there is a step-by-step description of the procedure for that activity. This is followed by answers where appropriate, possible variations and suggested follow-up.

All the timings are approximate and will vary depending on the group.

Many of the activities include sample material in boxes which you can photocopy and take into the classroom or simply use as a model to create your own material. You may, of course, prefer to put the material on the board or use an OHP.

I hope that you enjoy them.

Note

The majority of the examples in this book are taken from the *Cambridge Advanced Learner's Dictionary* and the *Cambridge Learner's Dictionary*. We have used the abbreviated forms *CALD* and *CLD* in this book.

1 Confidence and dictionary skills-building activities

This chapter has a range of activities to help learners understand how monolingual learner dictionaries work. The idea is to help them get used to the features of good learner dictionaries so that they can get the most out of them.

Many of the activities are aimed at lower-intermediate learners, who may be less familiar with how dictionaries work and need more help with basics like alphabetical order.

There are also activities which are suitable for learners with a higher language level such as 1.13 Navigating the dictionary: Using guidewords and signposts 2, and 1.14 Locating multi-word items.

The main thing is to try to get learners using dictionaries happily and comfortably. A little dictionary work, and often, is the key to learner independence.

1.1 Getting to know your dictionary

Aim	To familiarize students with dictionary features
Focus	Parts of a dictionary entry
Level	Lower-intermediate and above
Time	10 minutes
Preparation	Prepare an entry with features (usually found in the front of a dictionary) or use the one below from *CLD*.

Procedure

1 Ask students what information can be found in a learner's dictionary. Elicit:
   - meanings of words/definition
   - grammar information
   - pronunciation.

   (You can supply other types of information such as style – formal or informal, pictures, study pages, etc. or let students discover that for themselves in the next stage.)

2 Ask students to use the 'How to use this dictionary' section in the front of their dictionaries to label the parts of the entry below.
   a common errors
   b cross-reference to other information
   c example of word used in a sentence
   d part of speech
   e pronunciation of the word
   f shows that this is a common, important word

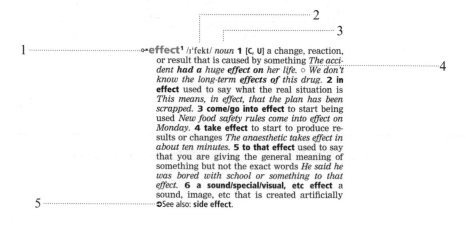

effect¹ /ɪˈfekt/ *noun* 1 [C, U] a change, reaction, or result that is caused by something *The accident **had a** huge **effect on** her life.* ○ *We don't know the long-term **effects of** this drug.* **2 in effect** used to say what the real situation is *This means, in effect, that the plan has been scrapped.* **3 come/go into effect** to start being used *New food safety rules come into effect on Monday.* **4 take effect** to start to produce results or changes *The anaesthetic takes effect in about ten minutes.* **5 to that effect** used to say that you are giving the general meaning of something but not the exact words *He said he was bored with school or something to that effect.* **6 a sound/special/visual, etc effect** a sound, image, etc that is created artificially ⊃See also: **side effect**.

6

> ### Common Learner Error
>
> **affect** or **effect**?
> Be careful not to confuse these two words.
> **Affect** is a verb which means to cause a change.
> *Pollution seriously affects the environment.* 6
> Use the noun **effect** to talk about the change,
> reaction, or result caused by something.
> *Global warming is one of the effects of pollution.*

Answers
1f, 2e, 3d, 4c, 5b, 6a

1.2 Finding the words you want quickly 1

Aim	To practise putting words in alphabetical order
Focus	Words that begin with different letters
Level	Pre-intermediate–Lower-intermediate
Time	10 minutes

Procedure

1 Explain to the students that they need to be able to look words up quickly, so they need to know how to use alphabetical order quickly. A very good way to practise this is to <u>put</u> words into alphabetical order.

2 Ask the class to dictate the alphabet to one student, who writes it vertically down the middle of the board. This is for them to refer to during the activity.

3 Explain that if all the words in the list begin with a different letter, you simply follow the order of the alphabet.

4 Either use the lists below or similar groups of eight to ten words that you have recently introduced. Put the words on the board or an OHT and ask students to put them in alphabetical order quickly.
   - one, two, four, six, eight, nine, second, last
   - colour, red, yellow, green, orange, white, blue

1.3 Finding the words you want quickly 2

Aim	To practise putting words in alphabetical order
Focus	Words that begin with the same letter, or same two letters
Level	Pre-intermediate–Lower-intermediate
Time	10–15 minutes
Preparation	Prepare lists of words you want the students to alphabetize, or use the lists below.

Procedure

1 If you did not use activity 1.2, explain the need to be able to look words up quickly: to do this, you need to know how to use alphabetical order quickly. A very good way to practise this is to <u>put</u> words into alphabetical order.

2 Ask students to dictate the alphabet to one student, who writes it vertically down the middle of the board. This is for them to refer to during the activity.

3 Explain that if all the words in the list begin with the same letter, they are alphabetized by their second letter.

4 Give students these words or a group of words you would like them to work on.

all   at   ask   and   about   age   ace   add

5 In groups, students race to put the words in alphabetical order and shout out when they think they've done it.

Explain that if all the words in the list begin with the same two letters, they are alphabetized by their third letter. Give students these words or a group of words you would like them to work on.

pad   pat   pass   pan   pain   page   paper

6 In groups, students race to put the words in alphabetical order and shout out when they think they've done it.

1.4 Spellcheck

Aim	To practise using alphabetical order to check spelling
Focus	Common spelling errors
Level	Intermediate and above
Time	10 minutes
Preparation	Prepare pairs of words (one correctly spelled, the other incorrectly spelled) or use the pairs in Box 1.

Procedure

1 Ask students to work in pairs or groups of three, sharing a dictionary.
2 Give students the words you have targeted and ask them to use their dictionaries to find which word in each pair is spelled correctly.
3 Check the task as a whole class activity

Box 1

Which word in each pair is spelled correctly?

1	a patience	b patiense
2	a recieve	b receive
3	a measurd	b measured
4	a simpliphy	b simplify
5	a recycel	b recycle
6	a ordinary	b ordinery
7	a communicasion	b communication
8	a severel	b several
9	a uncomfortible	b uncomfortable
10	a accommodation	b accomodation

© Cambridge University Press 2007

Answers (Box 1)
1a, 2b, 3b, 4b, 5b, 6a, 7b, 8b, 9b, 10a

1.5 Alphabet warmer

Aim	To practise the alphabet
Focus	Alphabetical order
Level	Elementary and above
Time	5 minutes

Procedure

1 Ask students how well they really know the alphabet.
2 Put students into groups and start going through the alphabet as a whole class activity.
3 After you've gone through the alphabet once, say that you're going to do it this time as a chain, with groups taking just parts of the alphabet.

4   Indicate one group to start. Stop them after a few letters, then signal that another group should take over from the next letter.
5   Go through the alphabet three or four times, speeding up.

Note
This can result in a bit of mayhem, but it is fun and a good warm-up activity.

1.6   Alphabet practice: Code breaking

Aim	To reinforce alphabetical order
Focus	Alphabetical order
Level	Elementary–Intermediate
Age:	May be more suitable for younger learners, although many adult students enjoy this activity
Time	10–15 minutes
Preparation	Prepare a few sentences for your students using simple codes that help reinforce alphabetical order, for example the letter before the letter (i.e. 'a' becomes 'z'), or the letter after (i.e. 'a' becomes 'b'). Or use the coded messages below (these are silly jokes but they are fun).

Procedure

1   Tell students that you have some coded messages and they need to find out what the messages say. The code for the first message is that it has been written using the letter just BEFORE each letter. The code for the second message is that it has been written using the letter just AFTER each letter.
2   Give out a copy of the first message or put it on the board or an OHT.
3   Give students time to work on decoding in their groups. When a group has successfully decoded the first message, give them the next one.

Message 1
Vghbg kdssdq hr mns ld?
T!

Message 2
Xijdi mfuufs jt bmxbzt uszjoh up gjoe sfbtpot?
Z!

Follow-up
Ask students to work in groups and think of a joke and put it in one of the codes for other groups to 'crack'. Or assign this as homework.

Answers
Message 1: Which letter is not me? U! (You)
Message 2: Which letter is always trying to find reasons? Y (Why?)

1.7 Navigating the dictionary: Where is the letter?

Aim	To practise locating letter sections in the dictionary
Focus	Alphabetical order
Level	Pre-intermediate–Lower-intermediate
Time	5–10 minutes

Procedure

1 Explain that in order to find words quickly, you need to be able find the letter of the alphabet the word starts with.

2 Point out that some letters of the alphabet have much larger sections, and more words in them, than others.

3 Dictate some letters of the alphabet, e.g. B, E, M, S, Y, and ask the students to predict which ones might begin the most words in English.

4 Compare the number of pages in the letter 'S' with the number of pages in the letter 'J' or 'K'. (If your dictionary has coloured letter tabs, ask students to have a look at the side of the dictionary.)

5 In pairs, or as a solo activity, students should try to find a letter by guessing where it is in the dictionary.

6 Write a letter on the board (C, P, S) then ask students to find it in the dictionary as quickly as they can and shout out the page numbers that letter begins and ends on as soon as they find it.

1.8 Navigating the dictionary: Where is the word?

Aim	To practise locating letter sections and words in the dictionary
Focus	Alphabetical order
Level	Pre-intermediate–Lower-intermediate
Time	10 minutes
Preparation	Prepare a list of words you want to recycle, or use the list on page 12.

Procedure

1 Write a word on the board, then ask students to find it in the dictionary as quickly as they can and shout out the page number as soon as they find it.

2 Use words that you want to recycle, or try this list (one word on the board at a time).

bench   courage   force   profile   squeal   wisp

Note

Remember, this activity is designed to get the students used to moving around the dictionary quickly and efficiently; they do not need to look at the definitions of the word at this stage.

1.9 Is that a real word?

Aim	To practise looking up words in the dictionary
Focus	Look-up skills
Level	Lower-intermediate and above
Time	10 minutes
Preparation	Prepare a list of real and 'invented' words, or use the list in Box 2. Make sure that at least some of the words are likely to be unfamiliar to your students.

Procedure

1 Tell students that they are going to use their dictionaries to find out which words are real (English) words and which are invented.
2 Check the task as a whole class activity.

Box 2

Which of these words are real English words, and which are invented? Put a tick ✓ in the column.

Word	Real	Invented
procrastinate		
cognitive		
jastle		
cumbersome		
retrivane		
frugal		
impunity		
simplistic		
eclectic		
misdrew		

© Cambridge University Press 2007

Variation

Ask students to work together in pairs or small groups and make lists for other groups. They need to check their 'invented' words as well as their real words to make sure that they are not, in fact, real.

They can also make a note of which page the real words are found on.

Answers (Box 2)

Real: procrastinate, cognitive, cumbersome, frugal, impunity, simplistic, eclectic

Invented: jastle, retrivane, misdrew

1.10 Navigating the dictionary: Parts of speech

Aim	To sensitize students to the fact that a word can be more than one part of speech
Focus	Parts of speech
Level	Lower-intermediate–Intermediate
Time	15–20 minutes
Preparation	Prepare a grid with words you want to present, practise or revise, or use the one in Box 3.

Procedure

1   Choose a word that can be more than one part of speech, for example, *open* or *stand*. Ask students to look it up and find out what parts of speech it can be.

2   Elicit the abbreviations used in your dictionary for parts of speech (noun, verb, etc. may be written in full, or the abbreviations *n.*, *v.*, *adj.* and *adv.* may be used).

3   Use the grid in Box 3, or create another one using words that you want to present, practise or revise. Ask students to find the words in their dictionaries and put a tick ✓ in the boxes to show which parts of speech each word can be.

4   Either in class, if there is time, or for homework, ask students to choose five words and write two sentences for each one, using the word as two different parts of speech. This can be done in pairs to make it more interactive.

Box 3

What part of speech can these words be?

	Noun	Verb	Adjective	Adverb
coat				
drink				
flat				
head				
junior				
slow				

© Cambridge University Press 2007

1.11 Navigating the dictionary: Labels

Aim	To familiarize students with dictionary labels
Focus	Style and usage labels
Level	Lower-intermediate–Intermediate
Time	15–20 minutes
Preparation	Check that the dictionary you are using labels the words on the list as in Box 4. If it doesn't, substitute suitably labelled words from your dictionary.

Procedure

1   Explain that learner dictionaries give us a lot of useful information about when and where to use a word or phrase.

For example, there are words that are formal or informal, words that are used mainly in literature or in specialized subject areas, and words that may be old-fashioned.

Because English has so many words that mean the same, or almost the same thing, this extra information helps language learners find the right word.

2   Use the list in Box 4 or dictate the list of words (saying and spelling the words, without the labels), or write them on the board or an OHT. Ask students to look them up in their dictionaries and find out what special usage labels they have. (This will vary from one dictionary to another, but any good learner dictionary will have labels. The list in Box 4 is based on *CLD*.)

3   Give students the lists and ask them to match the definitions with the label each describes.

Box 4

A Match the words with the labels.

Word	**Label**
1 abode	a *humorous*
2 freebie	b *formal*
3 hey	c *informal*
4 Hoover	d *literary*
5 slumber	e *old-fashioned*
6 snail mail	f *spoken*
7 wireless	g *trademark*

B Match the definitions with the labels.

1 formal

a a way of writing a word that is used in conversation

2 informal

b not used in modern English – you might find these words in books, used by older people, or used in order to be funny

3 spoken

c the name of a product that is made by one company but which has become used as a general word

4 trademark

d used in books and poems, not in ordinary conversation

5 literary

e used in order to be funny or make a joke

6 humorous

f used in serious writing or for communicating with people about things like business or law

7 old-fashioned

g used when you are speaking or communicating with people you know but not normally in serious writing

Answers (Box 4)
A 1b, 2c, 3f, 4g, 5d, 6a, 7e
B 1f, 2g, 3a, 4c, 5d, 6e, 7b

1.12 Navigating the dictionary: Using guidewords and signposts 1

Aim	To introduce using guidewords to find the right sense of a word
Focus	Recognizing guidewords
Level	Lower-intermediate–Intermediate
Time	15–25 minutes (the longer time will be required if word lists are dictated)
Preparation	Either use the lists in Box 5 (based on *CLD*) or create a similar list of multi-sense headwords (*case, drive, line*, etc.) and a list of their guidewords or signposts for students to work from.

Procedure

1   Explain that it often saves time if you try to guess the general meaning of a word before looking it up. This can be especially helpful when we come across words with several possible meanings. We use other words in the sentence to help us decide which guideword to use.
2   Then either give out the lists, write the headwords and guidewords on the board or, for a more challenging activity, dictate each list individually.
3   Students work together in groups to complete the activity using their dictionaries.
4   To consolidate the introduction to guidewords, go on to Activity 1.13, which practises using guidewords in context.

Box 5

Using guidewords

Use your dictionary to put the guidewords under the correct headword.

Headwords			
charge	**green**	**head**	**note**
——			
——	——		
——	——	——	

Guidewords

accuse	explanation	mind
ask to pay	feeling	money
attack	front/top	music
body	grass	not experienced
colour	information	organization
environment	letter	school

© Cambridge University Press 2007

Answers (Box 5)

charge	green	head	note
ask to pay	colour	body	letter
accuse	environment	mind	information
attack	grass	organization	explanation
	not experienced	school	feeling
		front/top	music
			money

1.13 Navigating the dictionary: Using guidewords and signposts 2

Aim	To practise using guidewords to look up the correct headword
Focus	Using context clues within a sentence to guess the general meaning of a word and decide which guideword to use
Level	Upper-intermediate and above
Time	15 minutes + 5–10 minutes feedback
Preparation	Either use the sentences and guidewords in Box 6 (from *CALD*) or prepare your own.

Procedure

1 Explain that it often saves time if you try to guess the general meaning of a word before looking it up. This can be especially helpful when we come across words with several possible meanings. We use other words in the sentence to help us decide which guideword to use.

2 Give students the sentences and possible guidewords.

3 Students complete the activity alone or in pairs.

4 Students check their answers using the guidewords or signposts in the dictionary.

5 Go through the answers as a whole class activity. Ask students to explain which other word(s) in the sentence they used to point them to the correct guideword.

Box 6

Which word?

Use the context clues to decide which guideword to use for the word in **bold**.

1 It was late so we decided to **head** straight for the station.
   a leader   b go   c top part   d mind

2 This tastes great. What did you **season** it with?
   a harden wood   b flavour   c part of year

3 All the paintings are interesting but I'm especially **drawn** to the one over there.
   a picture   b pull   c attract   d take out

4 The nurse **dressed** the wound and released him from the hospital.
   a shop window   b salad   c put on clothes   d injury

5 Pass me that **fork**, I want to dig this weed up.
   a food   b garden   c division

6 We're so **late**, I hope they'll let us into the concert.
   a near the end   b dead   c after

7 A **cake** of soap is a luxury in some parts of the world.
   a food   b shape   c cover

8 I can't **face** spending a whole weekend with them.
   a turn toward   b respect   c deal with

© Cambridge University Press 2007

Answers (Box 6)
1b, 2b, 3c, 4d, 5b, 6c, 7b, 8c

1.14 Locating multi-word items

Aim	To practise finding multi-word items in the dictionary
Focus	Phrasal verbs
Level	Intermediate and above
Time	25 minutes + 5–10 minutes feedback
Preparation	Prepare a number of sentences using phrasal verbs that you want to practise. These can be phrasal verbs that have already been presented or you can use this activity to present the phrasal verbs. Make certain that the target phrasal verb is clear from the context of the sentences. Alternatively, you can use the sentences in Box 7. It is important that students already understand that the meaning of phrasal verbs is not obvious. It is not easy to guess the meaning accurately even if you know the meaning of each part (word) of the phrasal verb.

Procedure

1 Explain that in most learner dictionaries phrasal verbs are found after the entry for the main verb. For example, the phrasal verb *find out* is defined after all the meanings of *find*.
2 Give students the sentences. You can supply a list of the missing items separately for lower level groups (see Box 7) but you may want to omit the list for higher levels.
3 Students complete the sentences in pairs or groups of three.
4 Check the task as a whole class activity.

Box 7

Look it up!

Use the dictionary to fill in the missing word in each sentence.

| into | off | on | out | over | through | up | up | (optional) |

1 If you can't get _____ to her mobile, send her an email.
2 We ran _____ an old friend last week.
3 He made _____ a story about the dog eating his homework.
4 Have you ever tried to give _____ smoking?
5 Remember to log _____ when you've finished using the computer.
6 Let's go _____ the story one more time.
7 I tried _____ several pairs of shoes before I found a pair that fitted.
8 She picked _____ a red shirt for me to wear.

© Cambridge University Press 2007

Follow-up

1 Encourage students to enter the phrasal verbs in their notebooks with the following information:

Phrasal verb	Meaning	Used in a sentence	Separable / Non-separable	Translation
get through	succeed in talking to someone	*I tried to call earlier but I couldn't get through.*	N	
pick out	choose	*We picked something out for each child.*	S	

2   Ask them to write sentences about themselves using the phrasal verbs.

Answers (Box 7)
1 through   2 into   3 up   4 up   5 off   6 over   7 on   8 out
(If you do not supply the missing words, students may find acceptable alternatives.)

1.15 Definitions

Aim	To practise recognizing differences in definitions of similar words
Focus	Definitions
Level	Intermediate
Time	10 minutes
Preparation	Either use the words and definitions in Box 8 or create your own.

Procedure

1   Give students the words and definitions.
2   Tell them that these words all mean *tell* but that they are used for different purposes.
3   Ask them to use their dictionaries to match the words and definitions.

Box 8

Match the words and definitions.

1 announce
2 brief
3 confide
4 divulge
5 relate
6 report

a   to give a description of something or information about it to someone
b   to give someone instructions or information about what they should do or say
c   to make something secret known
d   to state or make known, especially publicly
e   to tell a story or describe a series of events
f   to tell something secret or personal to someone whom you trust not to tell anyone else

© Cambridge University Press 2007

Answers (Box 8)
1d, 2b, 3f, 4c, 5e, 6a

1.16 Example sentences

Aim	To practise using example sentences to find the 'right' word
Focus	Example sentences
Level	Intermediate and above
Time	10 minutes
Preparation	Either use the words and example sentences in Box 9 or create your own.

Procedure

1   Tell students that example sentences in learner dictionaries are very useful. They show how to use the word in a sentence, and also make the definition clearer.

2   Give students the words and sentences and ask them to use their dictionaries to check the meanings of each word.

3   Students decide which word to put in the blanks. (They are all verbs so they may need to change the form.)

Box 9

Choose one word to complete the sentences. You may need to change the form.

announce	brief	confide	divulge	relate	report

1 They _____ the death of their mother in the local paper.
2 We rang the insurance company to _____ the theft.
3 She _____ the events of the previous week to the police.
4 Journalists do not _____ their sources.
5 We had already been _____ on what the job would entail.
6 He _____ to her that his hair was not his own.

© Cambridge University Press 2007

Answers (Box 9)
1   They *announced* the death of their mother in the local paper.
2   We rang the insurance company to *report* the theft.

> 3 She *related* the events of the previous week to the police
> 4 Journalists do not *divulge* their sources.
> 5 We had already been *briefed* on what the job would entail.
> 6 He *confided* to her that his hair was not his own.

1.17 Dictionary quiz

Aim	To familiarize students with their dictionaries or consolidate dictionary skills covered earlier
Focus	General dictionary skills
Level	Intermediate and above
Time	15 minutes (with feedback)
Preparation	Either prepare a quiz or use the one in Box 10 (based on *CALD*).

Procedure

1 Use this as a review of previous activities from this book, to familiarize students with a new dictionary or as a diagnostic quiz to decide which dictionary skills to target.
2 Students work in pairs or groups of three using one dictionary to answer the questions.
3 Check the answers as a whole class activity.

Variation

Make the quiz into a race – students work alone, and the first to complete the quiz correctly wins.

Answers (Box 10)
A 1d, 2c, 3a, 4b
B 1c, 2a, 3b, 4d
C 1a, 2d, 3b, 4c (puts them across)
D 1 real – adjective   2 invented   3 real – verb   4 invented
   5 real – noun   6 real – verb   7 real – noun, verb   8 real – noun
   9 real – verb   10 real – verb, noun

Box 10

Dictionary quiz

A Guidewords

Which is the headword for each of these groups of guidewords?

1 enjoy, game, act, move	a cone
2 competition, stick, suitable, equal	b heavy
3 shape, tree, food	c match
4 solid, man, to a great degree	d play

B Labels

Which of these words might be used as follows?

a amortize	**1** To make a joke or be funny about feelings
b Barbour	**2** When you are talking about money in a formal situation
c lurve	**3** To describe a type of coat
d plonk	**4** To describe wine to a friend

C Finding multi-word items

Choose the correct phrasal verb. You may have to change the form.

1 How long did it take you to_____ the flu?
2 It's an excellent film but it's quite complicated – there's a lot to _____ .
3 He said he was going to quit but I never thought he'd _____ it.
4 She has some interesting ideas and she _____ them _____ well.

a get over
b go through with
c put across
d take in

Dictionary Activities

D Real or invented?

Are these words real or invented? If the word is real, write the part of speech.

Word	Real (R) / Invented (I)	Part of speech
1 abject		
2 bast		
3 betray		
4 commention		
5 eyrie		
6 haggle		
7 notch		
8 smattering		
9 snuggle		
10 warble		

2 Vocabulary-building activities

Dictionaries, if nothing else, are books full of words, and the potential they offer for vocabulary development is enormous. The 20 activities in this chapter do not exhaust all the possible vocabulary-building dictionary activities, but they represent the most adaptable and are all tried and tested.

They are, like all the activities in this book, meant to be easy to use and to adapt. For example, you may prefer to use activity 2.2, which is based on pelmanism, with collocations, or with prefixes and suffixes, or with translations (which students can create using bilingual dictionaries) instead of words and definitions. The basic formula works every time.

Feel free to adapt, experiment, mix and match.

2.1 Learner training: Recording vocabulary

Aim	To record new vocabulary effectively
Focus	Lexical sets, word families, scales, word stress and silent letters
Level	Lower-intermediate and above
Time	30–40 minutes depending on the number and familiarity of the words used
Preparation	Prepare word lists or use the examples in Box 11.

Procedure

1   Start the lesson by asking students to describe the systems they use to record and revise vocabulary. Make the distinction between recording and revising (or reviewing) clear.

2   Elicit the type of information that you need in order to really 'know' a word (meaning, part of speech, spelling, pronunciation, usage and collocations).

3   Explain that there are different 'tricks' to help make vocabulary memorable and that you're going to practise some.

4   **Word groups (lexical sets)**
First explain that it is easier to remember words that are grouped by topic areas. Take a topic that you have covered recently. Put that topic on the board and brainstorm related words. For example:

	health	
doctor	symptoms	disease
nurse	ill	cure
patient	vitamin	injury

Give groups a list of words including the 'main' topic words in **bold**. (The list in Box 11 was created using *CALD*.) Ask them to put the words into three topic groups, looking up any words they're not sure of in the dictionary.

Box 11

Put the words into three topic groups.

acid rain	**environment**	journey	savings
bank rate	excursion	landfill	single ticket
biodegradable	expedition	layover	stock market
capital	finance	long-haul	stopover
commute	flight	**money**	**travel**
day trip	funds	oil slick	trip
deforestation	global warming	outing	venture capital
eco-friendly	green	pollution	voyage
ecosystem	greenhouse gas	recycle	
ecotourism	interest	return ticket	

© Cambridge University Press 2007

---

5 **Word families**

Explain that recording the various forms of a base word, or word family, is a powerful and efficient way to learn and record new vocabulary. Give each group two or three base words such as *argue*, *create* and *produce* and ask them to use their dictionaries to complete a table like this.

Verb	Noun	Adjectives / participles	Adverbials
destroy			

6 **Scales**

Explain that sometimes putting words on a scale is the most effective way to record words that are related in a different way. Scales are visual and make revision quick, easy and memorable.

Illustrate the way scales can be used by putting a scale on the board with 0% at one end and 100% at the other. Then add 'anchor' words like *never* and *always* in the adverbs of frequency scale. Either elicit or put a list of possible additions to one side (*rarely, sometimes, hardly ever, often, seldom*, etc.). Ask students to tell you where to put each item.

0%	100%
never	always

Give groups sets of words to put onto scales, using their dictionaries. Possible sets include: **temperature** (*cool, warm, hot, cold, boiling, scalding, freezing*), **angry** (*annoyed, furious, seething, cross*), **happy** (*pleased, morose, miserable, cheerful, radiant, ecstatic, delighted, sad, down*).

Ask each group to present their scales to the rest of the class.

7 **Word stress and pronunciation**

Explain that it is important to record word stress and pronunciation notes. Write several multi-syllable words on the board and mark the word stress as a whole class activity. Encourage students to use their dictionaries.

Then put a list of words with silent letters on the board (*island, lamb, calf*, etc.) and ask the students to tell you which letters are silent. Put a faint line or squiggle through the silent letters: *island, lamb, calf*.

8 Give students sets of recently learned vocabulary items and ask them to work in groups to decide which of the techniques they would choose to record them. Discuss their choices as a whole class.

Answers (Box 11)

Environment: acid rain, biodegradable, deforestation, eco-friendly, ecosystem, ecotourism, global warming, green, greenhouse gas, landfill, oil slick, pollution, recycle

Money: bank rate, capital, finance, funds, interest, savings, stock market, venture capital

Travel: commute, day trip, excursion, expedition, flight, journey, layover, long-haul, outing, return ticket, single ticket, stopover, trip, voyage

2.2 Definitions writing, matching and concentration

Aim	To learn new vocabulary or review and practise recently learned vocabulary items
Focus	Definitions
Level	Intermediate and above
Time	25–45 minutes depending on group size and number of words
Preparation	If possible, you will need pieces of coloured card or paper, about postcard size, enough for 10–20 pieces for each group.

Procedure

1 Put students into groups of three or four.
2 Give each group a list of five to ten words. If it is available, distribute 10–20 pieces of coloured card or paper to each group. (It is easier to keep track if each group has a different colour.) If not, ask them to use notebook paper.
3 Students look up the words, and then write the word on one card/paper and a short definition on another, using one side of the card/paper only. Monitor and check for errors. (Note: It does not matter if students copy the definitions directly; the activity will still provide useful exposure to the words and their definitions.)
4 When you are satisfied with the definitions, swap the sets of cards.
5 Students first match the words and definitions as a group.
6 Then they spread the cards out face down in rows and play 'Concentration' or 'Pelmanism'. The rules for this are:
   - Each person turns over two cards. If the two cards are 'a match', then they keep the cards and the next person takes a turn.
   - If the two cards do not match, the cards are returned to their original position (face down) and the next person takes a turn.
   - The person who takes the most tricks (matched pairs) wins.

Topic lists work well for this. For example:

Business and commerce
contract, deal, demand, e-commerce, export, import, market, profit, supply, tender

Environment
acid rain, biodegradable, bottle bank, ecosystem, environmentally friendly, greenhouse effect, habitat, landfill, pollution, recycle

Variation

When swapping cards in step 4, students who 'authored' the definitions can go to the group that has their cards and check that they have matched the words and definitions correctly before that group proceeds with the next stage. This helps you monitor for errors and reinforces the original group's grasp of the meanings of the words.

Topic lists can be created quickly either by the teacher or by the students as an extra challenge, using facilities like the Smart thesaurus on CD-ROM dictionaries.

2.3 Definitions bluff

Aim	To practise looking up and understanding words
	To learn (and teach) new vocabulary
Focus	Definitions
Level	Intermediate and above
Time	30–45 minutes depending on group size and number of words
Preparation	Prepare a number of cards, each with one word that you want to teach.

Procedure

1 Ask students to work in teams of three or four.
2 Give each group a list of words you want them to learn, preferably on cards, one word per card.
3 Ask the groups to look up each of their words and write out the definition. (If you are using this with an advanced group, you can encourage them to shorten the definition as much as possible.)
   They should also write out a second and, if you have time, a third definition which is false, for each word. Encourage them to use the dictionary for both the 'real' and the false definitions so that the false definitions sound authentic. Give them a time limit that is reasonable for the number of words you have given them.
4 Groups should then sit facing each other and take it in turns to show the word on their cards and read out their real and false definitions, to sound as convincing as possible. The other teams try to guess which definition is the real one.
   The defining team should then reveal which definition is the real one. Award the defining team one point each time they manage to fool the other teams.
   Encourage students to be cagey.

Note
This is based on a television programme called *Call My Bluff*.

2.4 Collocations 1: *Make* and *do*

Aim	To present verb + noun collocations
Focus	*Make* and *do*
Level	Intermediate and above
Time	15 minutes
Preparation	Prepare a list of *make* and *do* collocations or use the one below.

Procedure

1   Explain that in most learner dictionaries, the example sentences or fragments in an entry will contain other words that are frequently found with that word, i.e. their collocates.
    Tell students that it is a good idea, when learning new words, to learn their collocations and record them.
2   Either use the list of words below (based on *CLD*) or create your own list.
3   Either put the two words *make* and *do* on the board or an OHT and dictate the list to the students; or put the list on the board between the two words and ask students to use their dictionaries to put the words under *make* or *do* – this works well as a quick pairwork activity.
4   Check the answers together on the board.

make   do
                (someone) a favour
                a mistake
                an excuse
                (your) homework
                (a) noise
                the bed
                the washing-up
                your best

5   In pairs or groups, students work together to write a dialogue or story using all the collocates.

Note
Step 5 can be done as a competition – the group who uses all the collocations in one dialogue or story fastest wins.

> **Answers**
> make: a mistake, an excuse, (a) noise, the bed
> do: (someone) a favour, (your) homework, the washing-up, your best

2.5 Collocations 2: Verb + noun

Aim	To present verb + noun collocations
Focus	Verb + noun collocations
Level	Intermediate and above
Time	25 minutes
Preparation	Make one set of cards for each group of students (your own verb + noun collocations or using the list below).

Procedure

1 Make a list of vocabulary items you want to revise and extend or use the list below. Make cards (as below – one set per group of students), dictate the lists or write them on the board or an OHT.

2 Students work in pairs or groups to match a verb with a noun, using their dictionaries.

3 Check as a whole class activity.

cash	some advice
catch	a conclusion
change	a joke
keep	(a) cold
lose	a promise
reach	money
take	a cheque
tell	your temper

4 In pairs or groups, students write sentences or dialogues using the collocations, then remove the collocations and test other pairs or groups. For example:

Do you need to _____ a traveller's _____ ?

No, we _____ some _____ at the airport.

Let me _____ you two pieces of _____ :

Never _____ your _____ in an argument. You'll lose the
argument.

Always _____ your _____ .

Answers

cash a cheque (check), catch (a) cold, change money, keep a promise, lose
your temper, reach a conclusion, take some advice, tell a joke

---

2.6 Collocations 3: Adjective + noun dominoes

Aim	To present adjective + noun collocations
Focus	Adjective + noun collocations
Level	Upper-intermediate
Time	10–20 minutes
Preparation	Prepare a set of dominoes like the one in Box 12, with adjective + noun collocations.

Procedure

1 Put students into pairs or small groups. Give each pair or group a set of
dominoes and a dictionary.

2 Ask them to try to match up all the dominoes, starting with the one that
has the CHLT logo on the left. Remind them to use their dictionaries.

Box 12

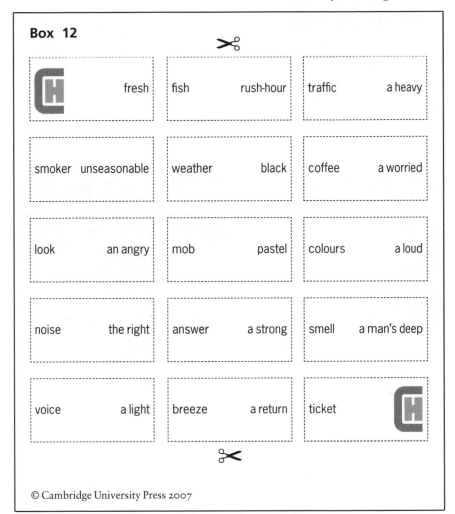

	fresh	fish	rush-hour	traffic	a heavy
smoker	unseasonable	weather	black	coffee	a worried
look	an angry	mob	pastel	colours	a loud
noise	the right	answer	a strong	smell	a man's deep
voice	a light	breeze	a return	ticket	

Note
This domino activity is very versatile and can be used with any type of collocation, and also phrasal verbs, idioms, etc.

2.7 Word building 1

Aim	To present and practise negative prefixes
Focus	Prefixes
Level	Intermediate–Upper-intermediate
Time	30–45 minutes
Preparation	Prepare lists of words of the same word class that take different negative prefixes – one list per group or pair. Alternatively, you may wish to use the lists opposite.

Procedure

1   Start by writing a familiar word on the board, for example *tidy* or *happy*. Ask students what the word means. Now ask how the negative is formed – add the prefix 'un'. Now write another word, one that takes a different negative prefix, for example, *possible* and elicit the negative.

2   Explain that learning negative prefixes is important because:
   • knowing how to use them is a quick way to increase active vocabulary
   • they are some of the most common prefixes
   • there are a few rules, but not many, and because there are exceptions to all of them, these words have to be learned.

3   Put students into groups. Give them the lists of words you have prepared or use the ones below. They will need to look up 'their' words, find out what they mean and what prefixes are used for each one. Ask them to write

two-line dialogues using both the base word and the negative. For example:

A: I think Luke is very mature for his age.
B: Oh no, he's very immature.

4 Form new groups, keeping one person from each original group. Ask students to 'teach' their words to the other students.

5 In conclusion, ask which negative prefixes they found. (The lists below yield 'un', 'im', 'il', 'ir', 'dis', 'mis' and 'in'.)
Tell them that it is a good idea to make a note of the negative (or opposite) when they are learning a new vocabulary item.

1	2	3	4
fortunate	able	necessary	reasonable
patient	possible	mature	perfect
legal	legible	literate	logical
responsible	regular	replaceable	reversible
trust	like	honest	respectful
discreet	visible	expensive	adequate

Note

You may wish to take this a step further and ask them to try to find patterns that can be used as rules of thumb, or you may want to tell them yourself. For example, 'im' is used before <u>some</u> words beginning with 'p' or 'm', 'il' is used before <u>some</u> words beginning with 'l', etc. It is a good idea to emphasize that there are exceptions.

2.8 Word building 2

Aim	To present and practise other common prefixes
Focus	Prefixes
Level	Intermediate–Upper-intermediate
Time	30–45 minutes
Preparation	Prepare cards or a worksheet like the one in Box 13 for the matching activity. Alternatively, select only those prefixes you want to focus on in this lesson.

Procedure

1 Ask students to work in pairs to find prefixes in the dictionary and match them with their meanings. (*CLD* and *CALD* have the prefixes listed at the back in the endmatter.) You can decide whether to direct students to this list, or ask them to look up each one in the dictionary. Ask them to find an example of each prefix (not one that is used as an example in the entry or list).

2   Check as a whole class activity. Ask a student to act as scribe and write the additional examples of each prefix on the board as students give them.

Box 13

Prefix	Meaning
anti-	after
auto-	against
bi	before
co-	between or among
ex-	do again
inter-	extremely
micro-	false
mono-	former or out of
over-	half or partial
poly-	many
post-	of or by oneself
pre-	one or single
pro-	small
pseudo-	supporting or in favour of
re-	too much
semi-	two
sub-	under
ultra-	with or together

© Cambridge University Press 2007

3   Next, ask students to draw a bingo card grid with four rows and four columns on a piece of paper. It should look like this:

Explain that you are going to dictate some prefixes and that they should put them in the grid randomly. (There are 18 in Box 13, 16 will fit on this card.) Now students should tick the prefixes off as you read out the meanings (short definitions) of the prefixes. Students should shout BINGO! when they have a row, column or diagonal run of four boxes ticked.

Variation

Alternatively, you can treat this activity as a jigsaw, and ask each group of students to look up three or four of the words on the list and feed back their findings to the rest of the class.

Answers (Box 13)

anti-: against   auto-: of or by oneself   bi-: two   co-: with or together
ex-: former or out of   inter-: between or among   micro-: small
mono-: one or single   over-: too much   poly-: many   post-: after
pre-: before   pro-: supporting or in favour of   pseudo-: false
re-: do again   semi-: half or partial   sub-: under   ultra-: extremely

---

2.9 Word building 3

Aim	To introduce suffixes
Focus	Suffixes for occupations
Level	Intermediate–Upper-intermediate
Time	15–20 minutes

Procedure

1 Write *dream jobs* on the board. Ask students what job they would like to do, and what they would like to be if they could be anything in the world. Give an example yourself of something, e.g. an actor, a painter, a musician, a guitarist, etc.

2 Give them a minute to think about it. Help with any vocabulary. Then ask them what their dream jobs are and put each one on the board. (If you aren't getting the range of suffixes you want, ask them to be more specific. For example, if they say they want to be a musician, ask which instrument they'd like to play, e.g. *guitar → guitarist*, etc.)

3 Underline the suffixes, and explain that by adding '-er' or '-or' to a verb, we create a noun that means the person or thing that does that activity; by adding '-ist', '-an' or '-ian' we also create a noun that means a person who does or believes something.

4 Ask students to choose one of the jobs discussed (not their original dream job) and a famous (locally or internationally) person who does that job.

5 The other students first have to guess the job, and then the person.

2.10 Word building 4

Aim	To present and practise suffixes
Focus	Suffixes and word class (parts of speech)
Level	Intermediate–Upper-intermediate
Time	15–20 minutes
Preparation	Prepare a list of words that have suffixes you would like to present or practise or use the words in Box 14. Put the words on strips of paper. If there is a suffix with two or more similar forms (like '-able' and '-ible'), write two representative words on one slip.
	Also put a grid like the one in Box 14 on an OHT (you can use the board but an OHT is better because you can conceal what is in each square with a Post-it™ or piece of paper).

Procedure

1 Give out the strips of paper, one per person, per pair or per group, depending on how you would like the students to work.

2 Tell them that they are preparing for a team game to test their knowledge of suffixes – there are 15 different suffixes to find.

3 Ask them to use their dictionaries to find out what part of speech each word is, and write the word, the suffix, and the part of speech in their notebook. (In this way they will have a record and can add to it when they come across more suffixes.) When they have finished with a strip, they should swap with another student. Give them a time limit that you think is reasonable. Circulate and monitor.

4 When that stage of the activity is complete, put students into two teams. Show them the grid (see Box 14) on an OHT. Ask students if they have ever played this game before (known as noughts and crosses in the UK, tic-tac-toe in the USA). Elicit the object of the game (to get a row of three horizontally, vertically or diagonally). In this game, they will have to change words into a different part of speech, using a suffix to win a square.

Flip a coin to decide which team starts. The starting team can choose whether to be team 'X' or 'Y'. Ask the starting team to choose a square, and reveal what is in the square AFTER they have chosen. If they get the answer right, write X or Y in the square.

Continue until you have a winner or no one can play.

Box 14 ✂

ability	friendship
active	homeless
childhood	illness
connection, explanation	intention
creative	likeable
cultural	powerful
dangerous	purify
disappointment	trainee

✂

explain (form a noun)	**able** (form a noun)	**care** (form an adjective)
forget (form an adjective)	**create** (form an adjective)	**identity** (form a verb)
history (form an adjective)	**inform** (form a noun)	**class** (form a verb)

2.11 Word building 5

Aim	To build compounding vocabulary
Focus	Compound adjectives to describe character
Level	Intermediate–Upper-intermediate
Time	15–20 minutes
Preparation	Create sets of compounds or use the ones in Box 15. Cut them up so that each group will have a complete set.

Procedure

1   Ask students to work in groups. Give each group a set of all three compound groups.
2   Ask them to match the first parts of the adjective compounds to one of the participles.
3   Then ask them to try to match the compounds to the correct definition. They check their answers with the dictionary.
4   Students then individually write paragraphs about someone they admire or someone they do not admire, using at least one compound from each set.

Box 15

✂

hard		not influenced by emotions
big	headed	thinking that you are more important or more clever than you really are
hot		reacting to things quickly and without thinking carefully first
single		very determined to achieve something
broad		willing to accept other people's behaviour and beliefs
open	minded	willing to accept ideas or ways of behaving that are different from your own
narrow		not willing to consider ideas and opinions that are new or different to your own
kind		caring a lot about other people and always wanting to help them
hard	hearted	not caring how other people feel
soft		kind and often feeling sympathy for other people

© Cambridge University Press 2007

Follow-up

Give groups different adjectives or participles that work as operators for a group of compounds and ask them to use their dictionaries to make a similar activity. For example, compound adjectives to describe appearance: *-eyed, -haired, -dressed*.

2.12 Word building 6

Aim	To build compounding vocabulary
Focus	Compound adjectives and nouns
Level	Intermediate–Upper-intermediate
Time	15–20 minutes
Preparation	Make a list of compound adjectives which can be used to describe three or four categories of nouns like the ones in Box 16.

Procedure

1 Ask students to work in pairs.
2 Ask them to use their dictionaries to sort the adjectives into three categories: *clothing, household appliances* and *people*. (For higher level groups, do not give them the categories.) Some adjectives may work in more than one category.
3 Check the categorization as a whole class activity.
4 Focus on the appliance category and brainstorm a few compound nouns which could be included in that category: *vacuum cleaner, dishwasher, food mixer, washing machine, tin opener, coffee machine*, etc.
5 In pairs, students write sentences using compound nouns and adjectives, e.g. 'A vacuum cleaner is a labour-saving device.'

Box 16

Use your dictionary to put these words into three categories.

hard-wearing	space-saving
labour-saving	high-heeled
left-handed	round-necked
long-sleeved	remote-controlled
long-suffering	drip-dry
meat-eating	short-sighted
nail-biting	mass-produced
self-cleaning	well-behaved

© Cambridge University Press 2007

Follow-up

Students find ten more compound nouns in the classroom or school, e.g. *noticeboard, filing tray, mouse mat, computer desk, desk tidy*, etc. and write a description of the classroom or school.

Answers (Box 16)		
Clothing	**Household appliances**	**People**
hard-wearing	labour-saving	left-handed
long-sleeved	left-handed	long-suffering
high-heeled	self-cleaning	meat-eating
round-necked	space-saving	nail-biting
drip-dry	remote-controlled	short-sighted
mass-produced	mass-produced	well-behaved

2.13 Word families

Aim	To practise choosing the correct form of a word
Focus	Derivatives
Level	Intermediate–Upper-intermediate
Time	15–20 minutes
Preparation	Prepare a number of gapped sentences using different forms of a word or use the sentences in Box 17.

Procedure

1 Put a noun which will generate several forms, e.g. *product*, on the board. Circle it and draw lines out from it like this:

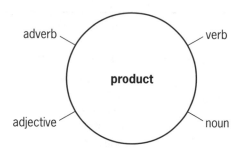

2 Ask students to work in groups and find at least one example of each part of speech in their dictionaries to complete the word family web. Give them a time limit of two or three minutes.

3   Elicit their answers and put them on the board (they could include: *produce v., producing v., produce n., production n., productivity n., productive adj., producing adj., productively adv.*).
4   Give them the gapped sentences. Tell them that all the gaps can be filled with words from one family.
5   Check together as a whole class activity, completing the word family web on the board.
6   Give each group a different base word to write similar word family gapped sentences for each other.

Box 17

Decide what part of speech each gap represents, then use your dictionary to find out which word family you need to use to complete the sentences.

profession	society	visit	investment	right

1 I chat to him at work but I never see him _____ .
2 I tend not to _____ with my colleagues.
3 I had an active _____ life when I was at college.
4 I had a headache and I wasn't feeling very _____ .
5 He was a _____ all his life.

© Cambridge University Press 2007

Note
For more advanced students, do not include the word box.

Answers (Box 17)
1 socially   2 socialize   3 social   4 sociable   5 socialite

2.14 Comparatives patchwork

Aim	To practise forming comparatives and superlatives
Focus	Comparatives and superlatives
Level	Any (the sample lists and the quiz in Box 18 are suitable for pre-intermediate–intermediate students)
Time	20–35 minutes (with step 1 of the Follow-up)
Preparation	Prepare a word list of items that you want to work on, grouped into three or four sub lists (see the sample list on page 46). The list should include regular and irregular items. For the Follow-up, prepare a quiz or use the one in Box 18.

Procedure

1 Give each student a master list of all the words, grouped into three or four sub lists.
2 Put students into groups and assign them a sub list. They are responsible for finding the comparatives and superlatives of all the words on that sub list.
3 Give students a time limit that is reasonable for the number of items on their sub lists.
4 When they have found their words, make new groups composed of one (or two, if you have a large class) student(s) from each group. They exchange their information so that each student has a full list of comparatives and superlatives.

Sample pre-intermediate master list

Sub list 1	Sub list 2	Sub list 3	Sub list 4
comfortable	bad	difficult	clever
early	easy	far	hard
good	fast	funny	important
long	frightened	late	modern
peaceful	hot	old	slowly
tall	narrow	quiet	well

Follow-up

1 Follow this up with a consolidation activity such as the comparatives quiz in Box 18 (pre-intermediate–intermediate level). This one also provides more practice in looking up words.
2 In groups, students use their dictionaries to write similar quizzes.

Box 18

Comparatives quiz

Use your dictionary to answer the following questions.

1 Which is bigger – a pond or a lake?
2 Which is longer – a river or a stream?
3 Which is older – a colt or a horse?
4 Which is hotter – tepid water or boiling water?
5 Which is later in the day – twilight or dawn?
6 Which is earlier in the day – dusk or noon?
7 Which is funnier – something that is amusing or something that is hilarious?
8 Which can run faster – a cheetah or a heifer?

© Cambridge University Press 2007

2.15 Adjectives: Positive or negative?

Aim	To build adjective vocabulary
Focus	People's personality and character, landscapes, feelings, food
Level	Intermediate and above
Time	20 minutes
Preparation	Either prepare a word list and categories or use the ones in Box 19.

Procedure

1   Start by brainstorming adjectives to describe people and their personalities or character. Organize your boardwork so that it will be easy to label the words positive (+) or negative (−).

2   Ask the students to look at the words you have brainstormed together and tell you whether they think they are positive or negative. (Or you can ask a student to do the labelling on the board.) Put a plus or minus sign next to each item. If they are neutral traits, put both (+/−) or 0. Opinions may vary.

3   Give students a list of words (on an OHT or on paper) to sort through, like the one in Box 19. Ask them to put them into categories. Put a simple grid on the board for them to draw in their notebooks or use the one in Box 19.

4   Look up a word together, e.g. *appetizing*. Discuss why this entry indicates a positive connotation in the *Food* category.

> **appetizing**, UK USUALLY -**ising** /ˈæp.ɪ.taɪ.zɪŋ/ *adj*
> describes food or smells that make you want to eat:
> *appetizing smells from the kitchen*

5   Check as a whole group activity. Discuss words that students categorized differently.

Follow-up

Ask which words on the list have a negative prefix (*irresponsible, undercooked, unspoilt*). Then ask them to find out which (if any) negative prefixes can be used with the other items.

Box 19

Use your dictionaries to put all the words on the list below into the grid. First put them into the correct categories, then use clues in the definition and example sentences to decide whether they are positive, negative or neutral.

People – personality and character			Feelings		
positive	negative	neutral	positive	negative	neutral

Landscapes			Food		
positive	negative	neutral	positive	negative	neutral

affectionate	enthusiasm	moody	savoury
appetizing	fear	patient	selfish
arrogant	filling	peaceful	sensitive
bitter	fried	picturesque	sour
bland	friendly	piquant	stodgy
bossy	generous	polite	stubborn
brave	honest	punctual	sweet
cheerful	imaginative	reliable	tasty
confidence	irresponsible	rich	undercooked
creative	jealous	rolling	unspoilt
cruel	jealousy	rude	vast
dry	lazy		

© Cambridge University Press 2007

2.16 Understanding connotation

Aim To strengthen understanding of connotation using dictionary definitions

Focus Connotations of near-synonyms

Level Intermediate and above

Time 20 minutes

Preparation Prepare a list of words or phrases which are near-synonyms with distinct connotations like the one below.

Procedure

1 Write the word *connotation* on the board. Ask students what it means (a feeling or idea that is suggested by a particular word). If they do not know, ask them to look it up.

2 Write *a slim person / a skinny person* on the board. Ask students what the connotations are for each word. Then ask them to look the words up to find out if their ideas were correct.

3 Look at the entries together. What words in the definitions give clues to connotation? (In the *CALD* entries below, the words are labelled 'approving' and 'disapproving', but in other dictionaries this may not be the case.) What other clues are there in entries? (Here: 'lovely' in the *slim* example sentence, 'too' in the *skinny* example sentence.)

> **slim** [THIN] ● /slɪm/ *adj* (slimmer, slimmest) APPROVING (especially of people) attractively thin: *slim hips/legs* ○ *She's got a lovely slim figure.* ○ FIGURATIVE *They've only a slim chance of winning* (= It's unlikely that they will win).
> **skinny** [THIN] /'skɪn.i/ *adj* MAINLY DISAPPROVING very thin: *You should eat more, you're much too skinny.*

4 Give students the pairs of words you have selected. (In the sample list here, one word or phrase in each pair has a more negative connotation than the other.)

5 Discuss the results as a whole class activity.

> **Sample list**
> someone who is well-known / someone who is infamous
> loud colours / bright colours
> a churchy person / a religious person
> an infantile attitude / a childlike attitude
> an unmarried woman / a spinster

Note

A quick and easy way to find words with strong negative connotations on the *CALD* CD-ROM is to use the 'disapproving' usage filter.

2.17 Multi-word expressions

Aim	To encourage students to learn the full range of expressions using a given word
Focus	Multi-word expressions
Level	Intermediate and above
Time	10–25 minutes (with the Follow-up)
Preparation	Either prepare gapped sentences that contain the same word in a number of different expressions or use the sentences in Box 20. (These are from the *CALD* example sentences.)

Procedure

1   Lead in to the area of expressions by eliciting a few expressions from a topic area you have been working on recently, e.g. *money*:
Money talks.
Money doesn't grow on trees.
Put your money where your mouth is.
2   Give students (in pairs or small groups) the gapped sentences (which are example sentences from *CALD*) and ask them to use their dictionaries to find the missing word. (For the sentences in Box 20 it is *moment*.)
3   Check as a whole class activity.

Follow-up

Groups use the dictionary model sentences to prepare similar 'expression gapfills' for the rest of the class.

Box 20

Which one of these words completes an expression in each sentence?

time	minute	place	moment	second

1 Help arrived, and not a _____ too soon.
2 I don't believe that story for a _____ .
3 Lift-off is always the _____ of truth for a new rocket.
4 I can give no information at this precise _____ in time.
5 Let's carry on with what we agreed for the _____ .

© Cambridge University Press 2007

2.18 Expressions: Opposites?

Aim To explore expressions and their meanings
Focus Pairs of 'opposites'
Level Intermediate and above
Time 10–15 minutes
Preparation Prepare a worksheet with pairs of words or use the one in Box 21. Choose pairs of words that have an opposites relationship in one sense, such as *absorb/reflect, expand/contract, join/separate.*

Procedure

1 Put a gapped sentence on the board that shows the opposites relationship of the two words and ask students to complete it. For example:
The colour black _____ light while the colour white _____ it.

2 Put students into groups. Give each group a different pair of words.

3 Ask students to use their dictionaries to find out which of the two words goes in column 2 of the chart.

4 Then ask them to complete column 1 of the chart with something that could form the subject of the expression, and write sentences for each expression.

5 When all the groups are ready, ask students to regroup in groups of three (depending on how many pairs you used) and exchange information.

Box 21

First decide which of the two words goes in column 2 of the chart, then complete column 1 with something that could form the subject of the expression.

absorb or *reflect*?

1	2	3
		a child's attention
		liquid
		information

1	2	3
		someone's face
		a change
		on the parents

expand or *contract*?

1	2	3
		on a topic
		knowledge
		the market

1	2	3
		malaria
		into the pension scheme
		cleaning out to a private company

join or *separate*?

1	2	3
		a sports club
		in the fun
		us later

1	2	3
		the north from the south
		from his/her husband/ wife
		the yolk from the white

Possible answers (Box 21)

Cartoons absorb a child's attention.
A sponge absorbs liquid.
Students absorb information.
A mirror reflects someone's face.
Statistics reflect a change.
A child's behaviour reflects on the parents.

A speaker goes on to expand on a topic.
Research expands knowledge.
New products expand the market.
Travellers to Kenya may contract malaria.
Most employees contract into the pension scheme.
Hospitals contract cleaning out to a private company.

Newcomers join a sports club.
Everyone likes to join in the fun.
We hope you can join us later.
The mountain range separates the north from the south.
She decided to separate from her husband.
Use a cup to separate the yolk from the white.

2.19 Phrasal verbs

Aim	To build phrasal verb vocabulary
Focus	Phrasal verb particles
Level	Pre-intermediate and above (the sample activity is upper-intermediate)
Time	15–25 minutes
Preparation	Choose a phrasal verb particle such as *up, back, through*, etc. that you want to present or revise. Prepare a set of gapped sentences which include various phrasal verbs formed with that particle, or use the ones in Box 22.

Procedure

1 Give students the sentences and the phrasal verbs and ask them to fill the gaps with the phrasal verbs, then check their answers in the dictionary.
2 Check again as a whole class activity.

3 Put the students into groups.

4 Give each group a particle. Ask them to use their dictionaries to write gapped sentences like the ones in Box 22. They can use the example sentences in the dictionary.

5 Groups swap sets of sentences and try to complete the gapfills, then check their answers in the dictionary.

Box 22

Complete each sentence with one of the phrasal verbs in the box. You will need to change some of the verb forms.
Check your answers in the dictionary.

> add up   blow up   bring up   come up   end up   fold up   move up
> turn up

1 _____ the figures and tell me what the total is.
2 By lap 26, Senna had _____ into second position.
3 Grandmother always _____ the TV when she comes in.
4 If you commit a crime you may _____ in prison.
5 Many parents have to struggle to _____ their children on a low income.
6 She _____ the newspaper and put it in her bag.
7 Something unexpected has _____ and we'll have to cancel the meeting.
8 The car _____ when flames reached its fuel tank.

© Cambridge University Press 2007

Answers (Box 22)

1 *Add up* the figures and tell me what the total is.
2 By lap 26, Senna had *moved up* into second position.
3 Grandmother always *turns up* the TV when she comes in.
4 If you commit a crime you may *end up* in prison.
5 Many parents have to struggle to *bring up* their children on a low income.
6 She *folded up* the newspaper and put it in her bag.
7 Something unexpected has *come up* and we'll have to cancel the meeting.
8 The car *blew up* when flames reached its fuel tank.

2.20 Common lexical errors: Correction

Aim	To encourage students to correct their errors using the dictionary
Focus	Various lexical usage errors
Level	Pre-intermediate and above (the sample activity is intermediate)
Time	10–15 minutes
Preparation	Collect lexical errors from your students' writing and speaking activities or use the common errors from *CALD* in Box 23.

Procedure

1 Choose a recent error your students have made, or this sentence from the Common learner error section in *CALD*: *I hope he doesn't loose his job*.

2 Write it on the board, tell students that there is an error and ask them to correct it using the dictionary.

   If your students are using *CALD* or *CLD*, they will find this Common learner error box:

COMMON LEARNER ERROR

loose or lose?

Be careful, these two words look and sound similar but have completely different meanings.

Loose is an adjective, meaning not fixed or not tight.

These trousers are a bit loose.

Lose is a verb, meaning 'to not be able to find something' or 'to have something taken away from you'. Be careful not to use **loose** when you really mean **lose**.

I hope he doesn't lose his job.
~~I hope he doesn't loose his job.~~

---

3 If their dictionaries do not have Common error boxes, ask them how they can decide which word to use. (They can check what part of speech it is, what the meaning is, etc.)

loose [NOT TIGHT] **A** /luːs/ *adj* (of clothes) not fitting closely to the body: *Wear comfortable, loose clothing to your exercise class.* **loosely** /ˈluː.sli/ *adv*: *The jacket hung loosely on his thin body.*
loosen /ˈluː.sᵊn/ *verb* [T] to make something less tight: *He loosened his tie.* **looseness** /ˈluː.snəs/ *noun* [U]

lose [NOT HAVE] **E** /luːz/ *verb* [T] (lost, lost) **1** to no longer possess something because you do not know where it is, or because it has been taken away from you: *I've lost my ticket.* ○ *He's always losing his car keys.* ○ *At least 600 staff will lose their jobs if the firm closes.* ○ *He lost his leg in a car accident.* ○ *She lost her mother* (= Her mother died) *last year.*

4 Ask students to work in pairs. Give out the sentences and ask them to correct them using their dictionaries.

Note
This activity can be used in conjunction with 3.9 Common errors: Transitive and intransitive verbs and 3.10 Grammar auction.

Box 23

Correct the errors in these sentences.

1 He's very sensible to other people's feelings.
2 All the children laughed after him.
3 I laid down and went to sleep.
4 The papers were laying on the table.
5 I wrote a letter to require more information.
6 Their office is in the 12th floor.
7 We discussed about the plans for the wedding.
8 Alex cried something to me across the street.

© Cambridge University Press 2007

Answers (Box 23)
1 He's very *sensitive* to other people's feelings.
2 All the children laughed *at* him.
3 I *lay* down and went to sleep.
4 The papers were *lying* on the table.
5 I wrote a letter to *request* more information.
6 Their office is *on* the 12th floor.
7 We discussed *(no preposition)* the plans for the wedding.
8 Alex *shouted* something to me across the street.

3 Grammar activities

Grammar and usage notes have improved a lot since they were first introduced in learner dictionaries. Old-style grammar codes were often convoluted and difficult to follow. In modern learner dictionaries, the trend has been to make them simpler and more transparent.

Of course, a lot of grammar information is presented or reinforced through the example sentences. Dictionary research has shown that students use example sentences as models and, although modern example sentences are often corpus-based, lexicographers keep clarity and intelligibility in mind when they choose which sentences to include.

3.1 Grammar codes

Aim	To introduce and practise using dictionary grammar codes
Focus	Various
Level	Any (the sample material is upper-intermediate)
Time	10 minutes
Preparation	Prepare a worksheet with grammar codes from the dictionary you are using or use the one in Box 24 (the examples are from *CALD*).

Procedure

1 Brainstorm parts of speech on the board, or write 'noun', 'verb' and 'adjective' on the board and elicit a few different types of each (noun – countable, uncountable, etc.).
2 Write *cat* on the board. Elicit what part of speech it is (countable noun).
3 Ask students to work in pairs and complete the worksheet.

Box 24

| alive | allot | apply yourself | deem | hitchhike | overwhelm | peace | vein |

Use your dictionary to decide which of the words in the box is:

1 a countable noun
2 an uncountable noun
3 an intransitive verb
4 a transitive verb that takes two objects
5 a reflexive verb
6 a verb that is not used in the continuous
7 an adjective that only follows a verb
8 a verb that is usually passive

© Cambridge University Press 2007

Variation
As a variant in step 3, you could set it up as a race.

Answers (Box 24)
1 vein 2 peace 3 hitchhike 4 allot 5 apply yourself
6 deem 7 alive 8 overwhelm

3.2 Countable and uncountable nouns

Aim	To follow up and practise countable and uncountable nouns and quantifier collocations
Focus	Countable and uncountable nouns, quantifiers
Level	Any (the sample material is intermediate)
Time	10 minutes
Preparation	Prepare a list of countable and uncountable nouns using the search facility on a CD-ROM or use the one in Box 25.

Procedure

1 Elicit a few countable and uncountable nouns and put them on the board.
2 Look them up in the dictionary as a whole group activity (either in a book-based dictionary, on CD-ROM or online) to see what grammar codes your dictionaries use.
  What other information does the entry give, e.g. collocations, usage notes?

3 Give students the list of nouns. Ask them to work in pairs to check the words in the dictionary and find out whether they are countable or uncountable.
4 Ask them to make a note of collocates for the uncountables, e.g. *roared with* laughter.
5 Ask pairs to check their answers with the pair next to them.
6 Elicit agreed answers and collocates. Ask whether there are any nouns which can be both countable and uncountable.

Box 25

Which of these are uncountable nouns?

advice	exit	outcome
air	fragrance	petrol
animal	gravity	product
answer	ground	salt
cable	information	sugar
cash	milk	water
egg	order	

© Cambridge University Press 2007

Possible answers (Box 25)
(Uncountables and collocates from CLD)
advice (some / a piece of)
air (some fresh air)
cash (short of cash)
gravity (centre of gravity)
ground (common / covered a lot of / on familiar)
information (some information about something)
milk (a carton of milk)
petrol (a litre / tank of petrol)
salt (a grain of salt)
sugar – both countable (*two sugars*) and uncountable (*a cup of sugar*)
water – a drink of water

3.3 **Uncountable nouns**

Aim	To practise uncountable nouns and quantifier collocations
Focus	Uncountable nouns
Level	Pre-intermediate
Time	10–20 minutes (with the Follow-up)
Preparation	Prepare a worksheet with uncountable nouns or use the one in Box 26. Either photocopy the worksheet, put it on the board or on an OHP.

Procedure

1 Elicit a few countable nouns.
2 Ask how they can be divided into 'amounts', e.g. *a kilo of sugar, a litre of milk*.
3 Look them up in the dictionary as a whole group activity (either in a book-based dictionary, on CD-ROM or online).
4 Give students the list of sentences. Ask them to work in pairs or groups of three and use their dictionaries to complete the task.
5 Check the task as a whole class activity.

Box 26

Which of the nouns in the box best completes each sentence?

advice	air	cash	gravity	information	petrol

1 We stopped at the first station we saw – we were nearly out of _____ .
2 Newton developed the laws of _____ .
3 Let me give you a piece of _____ – always mark the stress on new vocabulary.
4 It's hot in here. I've got to go out and get some fresh _____ .
5 Have you got much _____ with you?
6 Could you send me some _____ about the course?

© Cambridge University Press 2007

Follow-up

Give each group a list of four or five uncountable nouns and ask them to use their dictionaries to create gapped sentences like the ones in Box 26. Monitor and check. When they are ready, groups swap sentences and use their dictionaries to complete another group's sentences.

Answers (Box 26)
1 petrol   2 gravity   3 advice   4 air   5 cash   6 information

---

3.4 Recipes

Aim	To practise countable and uncountable nouns and quantifiers
Focus	Food
Level	Pre-intermediate
Time	15 minutes
Preparation	Create a recipe or use the one in Box 27. Check your dictionary to see whether you can use a picture page of quantities (as in *CLD* below) or whether students will need to look up the quantifiers in individual entries.

Procedure

1 Ask students if they like cooking. Ask if any are good cooks. Write *recipe* on the board. Elicit the meaning or look it up together. Ask whether they use recipes when they cook.

2 Show students the Quantities page from your dictionary or the section from *CLD* below.

3 Give students the recipe. Ask them to work in pairs or groups of three and complete the measurements of the ingredients using their dictionaries.

4 Check as a whole class activity.

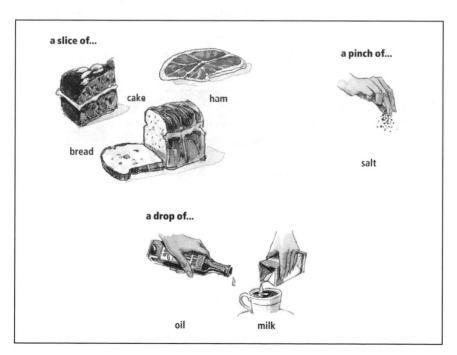

Box 27

Welsh rarebit
Ingredients

drops	grams	pinch	slices	tablespoon	tablespoons

100 _____ of cheddar cheese, grated
1 _____ of butter
a few _____ of brown sauce
2 _____ of milk
a _____ of salt
2 _____ of wholewheat bread

Instructions
Toast the bread.
Heat the cheese, butter and milk over a very low heat until it melts.
Spoon the mixture on the toast.
Sprinkle the sauce on the mixture.
Put the toast under the grill for just a minute until it is brown.

© Cambridge University Press 2007

Follow-up
Ask students to write out a recipe from their country for homework. Put the recipes together in a class collection.

Answers (Box 27)
100 *grams* cheddar cheese, grated, 1 *tablespoon* of butter, a few *drops* of brown sauce, 2 *tablespoons* of milk, a *pinch* of salt, 2 *slices* of wholewheat bread

3.5 Plurals

Aim	To recognize and practise noun forms
Focus	Nouns
Level	Upper-intermediate
Time	15 minutes
Preparation	Prepare a list of nouns or use the list in Box 28. Check the grammar codes in your dictionary before using this activity because it may use different codes.

Procedure

1 Give students the list of nouns. Ask them to work in pairs and try to put words into the appropriate categories *without* their dictionaries in the first instance.

2 Ask them to check their answers in the dictionary, then with another pair or group.

3 Ask them to try to put the words into the passages using context clues in the sentences.

4 Elicit possible clues (e.g. articles, plural/singular verbs, meaning, etc.).

5 Check as a whole class activity.

Box 28

A Put these nouns into the correct category. Then check them in your dictionary.

~~atmosphere~~	~~crisps~~	regulations	team
~~balance~~ (money)	government	resources	trousers
~~bacteria~~	media	rush	wait
binoculars	mess	scissors	
~~class~~	range	statistics	

1 Group	2 Plural	3 No plural	4 Usually plural	5 Usually singular
Noun which refers to a group of people or things and can be used with either a singular or plural verb	*Plural noun, usually used with a plural verb*	*Noun which can be used with a and an, but does not have a plural*	*Noun usually used in the plural form*	*Noun usually used in the singular form*
class	*bacteria*	*atmosphere*	*crisps*	*balance*

Now use the nouns from the table to complete passages B and C.

B

Our (1) _____ at school went on a bird watching trip one day. We were told to wear long (2) _____ . We were given a pair of (3) _____ , a packet of (4) _____ and a bottle of water.

We had quite a long (5) _____ before we saw anything exciting. Then one of the students opened his bag of (6) _____ and everything sort of happened in a (7) _____ : suddenly there were birds everywhere! Everyone panicked – it was a complete (8) _____ !

C

The (1) _____ is always issuing new (2) _____ to try and control the way we live. There seems to be a huge (3) _____ of bureaucrats with unlimited (4) _____ . They quote (5) _____ and tell us what's good for us. The (6) _____ then goes crazy and soon there's an (7) _____ of hysteria over nothing.

Follow-up
Students write a paragraph using two or three of the nouns.

> Answers (Box 28)
> A **1** class, government, media, team   **2** bacteria, binoculars, scissors, trousers   **3** atmosphere, rush, wait   **4** crisps, regulations, resources, statistics   **5** balance, mess, range
> B **1** class   **2** trousers   **3** binoculars   **4** crisps   **5** wait   **6** crisps   **7** rush   **8** mess
> C **1** government   **2** regulations   **3** team   **4** resources   **5** statistics   **6** media   **7** atmosphere

3.6 Dependent preposition wheels

Aim To practise dependent prepositions
Focus Adjectives
Level Intermediate and above
Time 25 minutes
Preparation Prepare a list of nouns and/or adjectives that are followed by a particular preposition or use the one in Box 29.

Procedure
1 Tell students that some nouns and adjectives are followed by particular prepositions.
2 Put a word like *surprised* on the board. Ask students to use their dictionaries to find out what prepositions usually follow *surprised* (*at* or *by*).
3 Ask them to put a diagram like the one in Box 29 on a page in their notebooks.
4 Explain that these are all common dependent prepositions.
5 Give them the list of words you want them to work with. Ask them to use their dictionaries to find out which adjectives are followed by which prepositions. Remind them that some of the adjectives may have more than one frequent dependent preposition.

Follow-up
Ask students to write sentences about themselves or people they know using ten of the adjectives + prepositions.

Box 29

Use your dictionary to find out which adjectives are followed by which prepositions.

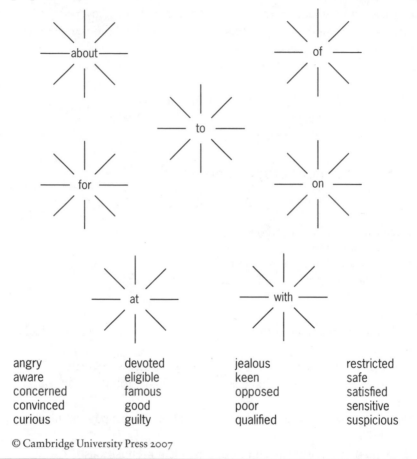

angry	devoted	jealous	restricted
aware	eligible	keen	safe
concerned	famous	opposed	satisfied
convinced	good	poor	sensitive
curious	guilty	qualified	suspicious

© Cambridge University Press 2007

3.7 Dependent prepositions: Error correction

Aim	To use dictionary entries to check grammar
Focus	Nouns and verbs + dependent prepositions
Level	Intermediate and above
Time	20 minutes
Preparation	Prepare a text with errors to correct or use the one in Box 30.

Procedure

1 Put a few nouns which frequently co-occur with dependent prepositions on the board, e.g. *attitude, intention*.

2 Ask students to look them up and decide what dependent prepositions they take (attitude *towards/to*, intention *of*).
Ask how they found the information (in the example sentences).

3 Give them the text. Ask them to work in pairs and use their dictionaries to correct it.

Box 30

There are ten errors (in *italics*) in this text. Use your dictionary to correct them.

Here at Happy Factories, we take *pride on* the fact that the management really *cares of* their staff. We feel this is the *key of* a good working environment.

We understand that some staff members did not *agree in* the salary cuts that we have had to make. The *reason of* the salary cuts was that it was the only *solution from* our financial problems.

As a *result from* the recent *increase of* sales, we are happy to tell you that employees may now *apply from* a new money purchase plan. If you are *interested on* joining the plan, contact your line manager.

© Cambridge University Press 2007

Follow-up

Students write either a short letter asking for information about a course, holiday or product OR a paragraph about a statement they agree or disagree with, such as: *Smoking should be banned from all public places.*

Answers (Box 30)
1 pride in   2 cares about   3 key to   4 agree with   5 reason for
6 solution to   7 result of   8 increase in   9 apply for   10 interested in

3.8 *to* or *-ing*?

Aim	To practise using the dictionary to correct and check grammar
Focus	Infinitives and gerunds
Level	Intermediate
Time	25 minutes
Preparation	Prepare a list of sentences which have gerund/infinitive specific verbs, some correct and some incorrect. (If possible, use verbs which the students have made errors with. These could be collected when you are monitoring a speaking task or from their written work.) Or use the party theme sentences in Box 31.

Procedure

1 Show students a dictionary entry like the one here for *enjoy* (from CLD). Draw their attention to the usage note and example sentence.

usage note ——

enjoy /ɪnˈdʒɔɪ/ *verb* [T] **1** If you enjoy something, it gives you pleasure. *I hope you enjoy your meal.* [+ doing sth] *I really enjoyed being with him.* **2 enjoy yourself** to get pleasure from something that you are doing *Everyone eventually relaxed and began to enjoy themselves.* **3** *formal* to have or experience something good such as success *His play enjoyed great success on Broadway.*

2 Give students the sentences. Ask them to work in pairs or groups of three and use their dictionaries to check which verb form is correct in each sentence.

Box 31

Which is the correct form?

1 We've been invited *to go / going* to a party.
2 I offered *to download / downloading* some music for the party.
3 Are we allowed *to bring / bringing* guests?
4 What time did you arrange *to meet / meeting*?
5 I dislike *to dance / dancing* – I'm a terrible dancer.
6 I overheard him *to say / saying* that they are leaving soon.
7 They have to hurry *to catch / catching* the last train.
8 There were lots of people queuing *to get /getting* tickets at the station.
9 Please consider *to take / taking* a taxi.
10 He asked me *to ring / ringing* when I got home.

© Cambridge University Press 2007

---

3   Working on their own or in pairs, students write sentences using these words: *busy, enjoy, difficulty, confidence, careful, decide*.

Follow-up
Students write a paragraph about something that they have always wanted to try – painting, snowboarding, diving, etc. – and why. Encourage them to use verbs!

Answers (Box 31)
1 to go   2 to download   3 to bring   4 to meet   5 dancing   6 saying
7 to catch   8 to get   9 taking   10 to ring

3.9 Common errors: Transitive and intransitive verbs

Aim	To practise using the common errors boxes in the dictionary
Focus	Transitive and intransitive verbs
Level	Intermediate
Time	15 minutes
Preparation	Prepare a list of sentences with verbs that your students have been having difficulty with, or use the sentences in Box 32.

Procedure
1   Show students the Common learner error box below (from *CALD*).

COMMON LEARNER ERROR

rise or **raise**?

Be careful not to confuse these two verbs. **Rise** means to increase or move up. This verb cannot be followed by an object.

The price of petrol is rising.
The price of petrol is raising.

Raise means to lift something to a higher position or to increase an amount or level. This verb must always be followed by an object.

The government has raised the price of petrol.
The government has rised the price of petrol.

2   Ask them to work in pairs and decide whether to use *rise* or *raise* in each of the sentences in Box 32, then check their decisions in the dictionary.
3   Check and discuss their answers as a whole class activity.
4   Discuss whether your dictionary indicates that any of these are expressions.

Box 32

Decide whether to use *rise* or *raise* in these sentences. You may need to change the tense in some cases. Then check your answers in the dictionary.

1 She_____ above her difficulties and became a successful businesswoman.
2 His answers _____ doubts in my mind.
3 I want to start my own business if I can _____ the capital.
4 Jemma's ideas _____ a few eyebrows.
5 Let's all _____ our glasses to the happy couple.
6 My spirits_____ whenever I think of my friends.
7 Never_____ your hand to a child.
8 Shall we _____ the issue of salaries?
9 She was_____ by her grandparents.
10 The discussions became heated as tempers began to _____ .
11 The people_____ up in rebellion against the dictator.
12 The sun _____ in the east.

© Cambridge University Press 2007

Answers (Box 32)

1 rose   2 raised   3 raise   4 raised   5 raise   6 rise   7 raise   8 raise
9 raised   10 rise   11 rose   12 rises

3.10 Grammar auction

Aim	To practise using the usage notes and/or study pages of a dictionary
Focus	This format is very adaptable. You can use it to work on virtually any language area. The activity is particularly useful as an error correction stage after a fluency activity.
Level	Any (the language can be graded as you see fit)
Time	30 minutes (more or less; it depends on the level of the class, number of sentences, number of teams, etc.)
Preparation	Prepare a list of ten sentences (more, if you have time), some of which are correct, others that contain at least one grammar mistake.

Procedure

1 Split the class into three or more teams. Ask each team to think of a name. (It is worth taking the time to do this as it provides motivation.)

2 Put the following grid on the board:

Team name	Number of correct sentences	Money left
		£1,000
		£1,000

3 Write the words *auction, bid* and *bidder* on the board. Ask students to use their dictionaries to find out what they mean and to use each word in a sentence. Ask them if they know of a famous local auction house or Christie's or Sotheby's in London.

4 Tell students that you have some excellent sentences in this auction. They are going to have a chance to bid for them. Each team starts with £1,000. The minimum first bid is £100, then they may bid in increments of £50. The winners are the team that has bought the largest number of correct sentences.

Tell students that they should use their dictionaries to check the sentences by looking up one or more key words. (These might be tenses, countable or uncountable nouns, dependent prepositions or any other grammar area that they have studied.)

5 Start the auction by writing the first sentence on the board. Start with either a correct one, e.g.
I would like some information about the course.
or an incorrect one, e.g.
I would like some informations about the course.

6 When the bidding is over, announce 'Sold – to team X.' Then deduct the amount that the successful team bid from their balance.

7 Finally, ask the whole class whether the sentence is correct or not. If it is a correct sentence, add a point to the owners' score under 'Number of correct sentences'. (If no teams bid for an incorrect sentence, you can offer half a point to the first team to correct the sentence and to give the dictionary reference – a usage note, study page or example sentence.)

Notes

1 It is a good idea to plan your boardwork so that you have plenty of room to write each individual sentence up as well as the team grid.

2 This is a dictionary variation of an activity that first appeared in *Grammar Games* by Mario Rinvolucri, 1985, published by Cambridge University Press.

4 Pronunciation activities

Learner (print) dictionaries usually provide the phonemic transcription of all headwords, mark word stress, and indicate differences in pronunciation across language varieties.

The activities in this chapter are designed to work with print dictionaries and are purposely low-tech but they can all be used with CD-ROM dictionaries, and several have tips on using CD-ROMs.

CD-ROM dictionaries differ quite a bit in terms of how they deal with pronunciation. Most now have a facility for students to record their own pronunciations and compare theirs with the model. (Activities using this facility have not been included because the focus here is on classroom activities, not on self-access ones.)

4.1 Syllables and stress

Aim	To practise using the dictionary to identify syllable breaks and word stress
Focus	Syllables and word stress
Level	Elementary
Time	25 minutes
Preparation	Prepare lists of words or use the ones in Box 33 (these are all food related). To create a topic list quickly and easily, use the picture pages in a print dictionary or the search facility on the CD-ROM. You may want to give each student a master list of all the words to make notes in the feedback stage. Check the pronunciation conventions used in the dictionary you are using.

Procedure

1 Write a few words from your topic area on the board. For example, *breakfast, lunch* and *dinner*. Ask students to use their dictionaries to find out how many syllables the words have and where the stress is in each word.

2 Draw stress patterns on the board and ask students where you should put each of the words. For example:

lunch

breakfast
dinner

3   Put students into groups. Assign a set of words to each group. Ask them to use their dictionaries to mark the syllable breaks and put the words under the correct stress patterns.

4   Ask groups to go to the board and present their results. Ask the whole class to say each word as they present its stress.

Box 33

Mark the syllable breaks and put the words under the correct stress patterns.

Food

biscuits	yoghurt	watermelon
banana	apple	carrot
butter	cauliflower	celery
cereal	coconut	cucumber
honey	grapefruit	lettuce
pasta	lemon	onion
pizza	melon	potato
salad	orange	sweetcorn
sandwich	pineapple	tomato
vegetable	strawberry	cabbage

A   B   C   D

© Cambridge University Press 2007

74

> Answers (Box 33)
>
> **A** biscuits, butter, honey, pasta, pizza, salad, sandwich, yoghurt, apple, grapefruit, lemon, melon, orange, carrot, lettuce, onion, sweetcorn, cabbage
> **B** cereal, vegetable, coconut, pineapple, strawberry, celery, cucumber
> **C** banana, potato, tomato
> **D** watermelon, cauliflower

4.2 Stress: Two syllable nouns and verbs

Aim	To use the dictionary to check stress and part of speech
Focus	Two syllable nouns and verbs
Level	Intermediate and above
Time	15–20 minutes
Preparation	Prepare a list of words or use the one in Box 34.

Procedure

1 Start by writing the word *answer* on the board. Ask students to tell you where the stress is. Then ask them to tell you whether it is a noun or a verb. (It can be both.) Does the stress change? (No, it doesn't.)

2 Now write *permit* on the board. (It can be both a verb and a noun. The stress changes.)

3 Ask students to work in pairs and work through the list using their dictionaries. (Both print and CD-ROM dictionaries are fine for this activity.)

Follow-up

Put the students into new groups. Ask them to use their dictionaries to create sentences for each word that can be both a noun and a verb.

Box 34

Complete the table with your answers.

- Where is the stress?
- Which of these words can be both a verb and a noun?
- Does the stress pattern change?
- Write whether the stress pattern is A or B.

Stress patterns

A

B

	Noun	Verb
allow	–	B
accent		
commit	–	
contract		
damage		
export		
flower		
forgive	–	
import		
level		
record		
release		
reply		
report		
weather		
wonder		

Answers (Box 34)

	Noun	Verb
allow	–	B
accent	A	A
commit	–	B
contract	A	B
damage	A	A
export	A	B
flower	A	A
forgive	–	B
import	A	B
level	A	A
record	A	B
release	B	B
reply	B	B
report	B	B
weather	A	A
wonder	A	A

4.3 *-ed* endings

Aim	To increase student awareness of the pronunciation of regular past verb endings
Focus	*-ed* endings
Level	Elementary–Intermediate
Time	15–20 minutes (more with the Follow-up)
Preparation	Prepare a list of regular past verbs or use the one in Box 35.

Procedure

1 Write three verbs that take *-ed* endings which are pronounced differently on the board. For example, *close*, *walk* and *want*.

2 Elicit their past tenses.

77

3   Write the three patterns on the board – see Box 35. Ask students where each verb should go.
4   Give students the list. In pairs or groups of three, students work together using dictionaries to put the verbs under the correct heading.
5   Check as a whole class activity. Elicit patterns that the students have seen emerge or give them the information in the Key.

Follow-up
In groups, students choose six to ten verbs and create a story using their chosen verbs and tell it to the class.

Box 35

1	2	3
◯ /t/	◯ /d/	◯◦ /ɪd/
walked	closed	wanted

added	learned	shouted
cleaned	mended	started
closed	missed	stopped
cooked	mixed	waited
counted	opened	walked
danced	painted	wanted
dreamed	phoned	watched
hired	played	
laughed	rested	

© Cambridge University Press 2007

Note

Before using this activity, check that the dictionary you are using shows the pronunciation of *-ed* endings.

Key (Box 35)

Pattern 1 follows these letters: - p - k - s - ch - sh - f - x - h

Pattern 2 follows these letters: - l - v - n - m - r - b- v -g - w - y - z

Pattern 3 follows these letters: - t - d

4.4 Homophones

Aim	To check spelling of common errors
Focus	Homophones
Level	Intermediate and above
Time	10–15 minutes
Preparation	Prepare a number of sentences that contain a homophone or use the sentences in Box 36. Write both homophones, one to be crossed out.

Procedure

1   Give students the sentences. Ask them to work alone, in pairs or in small groups as appropriate, and choose the correct spelling.

2   Either give students a time limit or make the activity a race to see who finishes first.

Box 36

Which word is correctly spelled in these sentences? Cross out the incorrect word.

1	That's a *great / grate* looking car! /greɪt/
2	There were *two / too* many children in the room. /tuː/
3	Do you want half an apple or a *whole / hole* one? /həʊl/
4	*Their / They're* usually late. /ðeə/
5	Let's *meat / meet* in front of the hotel. /miːt/
6	You *seem / seam* a little down – what's wrong? /siːm/
7	What time did you get *there / their*? /ðeə/
8	He hit the *breaks / brakes* and stopped just in time. /breɪks/
9	The *gorillas / guerrillas* have never been in contact with humans. /gərɪləz/
10	You really are a *site / sight* for sore eyes! /saɪt/

© Cambridge University Press 2007

Follow-up

Put each pair of homophones (the two spellings and the phonemic script) on a card. Put the class into teams. Teams take a card in turn and must produce two sentences – one for each homophone. Award a point for each pair of correct sentences.

Variation

If your students know IPA, you can write the homophone in phonemic script and ask them to write the correct spelling of the word.

4.5 Minimal pairs

Aim	To practise recognizing individual sounds
Focus	Vowel sounds (and spelling)
Level	Elementary–Pre-intermediate
Time	10—15 minutes
Preparation	Choose individual sounds that your students are having trouble with to create a list or use the words in Box 37. Make cards – one word per card, with enough cards for each pair or group to have a set.

Procedure

1 Put a minimal pair you want to work with on the board. For example, *pin* and *pine*.

   1 pin /pɪn/   2 pine /paɪn/

   Do a quick choral drill, pointing to each word as you say it.

2 Ask the students to tell you which one you are saying by shouting '1' or '2'. Turn your back to the students so that they can't see your mouth and continue.

3 Put the students into pairs or small groups and give them the cards. Ask them to use their dictionaries to sort the words into the appropriate group.

4 Check the task as a whole class activity.

Box 37

big	byte	dine	dish
fight	guide	height	hymn
kick	knit	tied	light
myth	rhyme	tip	type

© Cambridge University Press 2007

Variation

If you prefer not to make individual cards, give students the list of words and ask them to number the two groups, e.g. 1 big, kick, 2 fight, byte, etc.

4.6 Odd one out

Aim	To practise using the dictionary to check pronunciation
Focus	This is an adaptable activity. It is suitable for checking or practising word stress, individual sounds, diphthongs, -*ed* endings, etc.
Level	Any
Time	10–15 minutes (with the Follow-up)
Preparation	Prepare a list of words that practise individual sounds or use the one in Box 38. Either photocopy the list, put it on the board or on an OHP. (Dictation is not suitable for this activity.)

Procedure

1 If this is the first time you have used the activity, do one example once you have given them the words.
2 Ask students to work alone, in pairs or in small groups as appropriate. Either give them a time limit or make the activity a race to see who finishes first.

Box 38

Odd one out – Vowels
Circle the word that sounds different from the other two.

Example:

	a show	b (now)	c tow
1	a cough	b rough	c tough
2	a throw	b through	c threw
3	a sieve	b scene	c lift
4	a dough	b stow	c plough
5	a rhyme	b bright	c brief
6	a chime	b chill	c thyme
7	a ache	b act	c plain
8	a touch	b stuff	c couch
9	a sew	b grew	c glow
10	a fine	b sign	c rain

© Cambridge University Press 2007

Follow-up
Put students in pairs or groups and ask them to make a sentence using at least two of the words in each set. For example: *She threw her computer through the window.*

Variation
In groups, students can also make 'Odd one out' pronunciation activities themselves and test other groups.

Note
This activity is suitable for either using the phonemic script in a print dictionary or the sound and phonemic script on a CD-ROM.

Answers (Box 38)
1a, 2a, 3b, 4c, 5c, 6b, 7b, 8c, 9b, 10c

4.7 Rhymes?

Aim	To practise using the dictionary to check pronunciation
Focus	Vowel sounds
Level	Pre-intermediate–Intermediate (but can be adapted to any level)
Time	10–15 minutes
Preparation	Create pairs of sentences, some of which rhyme, others that don't, or use the ones in Box 39. Either make copies, one per pair, or put them on the board or an OHT.

Procedure

1 Write *rhyme* on the board. Ask students what it means and how it is pronounced. Then write a few pairs of words on the board, for example *so* and *throw, stuff* and *tough* and ask students to use their dictionaries to find out whether they rhyme or not.

2 Put students in pairs and ask them to use their dictionaries to decide which pairs of lines rhyme.

3 Check as a whole class activity, asking students to read out each pair.

Box 39

Use your dictionary to find out which pairs of lines rhyme.

1   Don't buy clothes that are new,
    Save your money and learn to sew.

2   Plant the seeds in a row.
    Put up a fence to keep out the cow.

3   Turn that down, for heaven's sake!
    It's giving me a bad headache.

4   The life of a mule is very tough.
    It carries wood and pulls the plough.

5   What would you like to do now?
    Let's go to London and see a show.

6   Do you know what I just heard?
    The lead singer is growing a beard!

7   He says he's turning over a new leaf,
    He's hoping they're going to make him chief.

8   Fred's a little out of touch,
    All he does is sit on the couch.

9   She has a sore throat and a cough,
    She says she's feeling really rough.

10 You know, it takes a lot of time
    To think of sentences that rhyme!

PLANT THE SEEDS IN A ROW.
PUT UP A FENCE TO KEEP OUT THE COW.

4.8 Rhyming slang

Aim	To practise using the phonemic transcription in the dictionary
Focus	Rhymes
Level	Intermediate and above
Time	20–30 minutes
Preparation	Prepare cards like the ones in Box 40, enough for each student to have one. Also prepare a short list of words for each pair or group.

Procedure

1 Explain Cockney rhyming slang to students. Some say that it was used as a 'secret language' in the markets and docks of East London. People still use some of the old slang. For example, *loaf of bread* = head; this is shortened to 'Use your loaf', and means 'Use your head.' People continue to invent new slang, e.g. *Calvin Klein* = wine.

2 Give students a card (or cards, depending on numbers) each. Ask them to stand up and mingle, saying their word or phrase out loud and listening for one that rhymes with theirs.

   When all the pairs have found each other, they should read out their phrase and its meaning.

3 Give out the lists you have prepared. Ask pairs to first look up each word in the dictionary, transcribe it into phonemic script, and then work together to find words (or very common phrases) to rhyme with each of the words they have been given and create their own 'slang'.

4 Circulate and monitor.

5 Feed back as a whole class.

Box 40

✂

plates of meat	feet
trouble and strife	wife
dog and bone	phone
apples and pears	stairs
china plate	mate
tea leaf	thief
loaf of bread	head
bread and honey	money
north and south	mouth
pork pies	lies

© Cambridge University Press 2007

Note

If students have access to a CD-ROM with a sound search facility, they can use that. They will still need to look up the phonemic transcription of the target words.

4.9 Bespoke tongue twisters

Aim	To locate, use and practise pre-selected individual sounds
Focus	Specific sound pairs
Level	Any
Time	10–15 minutes
Preparation	Prepare a set of target phonemes for students to work on. If you are teaching a multilingual class, think about the pronunciation problems

that the various language groups have, e.g. /l/ and /r/, /b/ and/v/, /w/ and /v/, etc.

If you have time, and access to a CD-ROM with a sound search facility like the *Macmillan Essential Dictionary*, you could also make some skeletal word lists (words that contain the target phonemes) for the students to add to. If the students have access to the CD-ROM, then so much the better. They can make their own word lists (see Note below).

Procedure

1 Introduce the concept of tongue twisters, either by putting one (such as *She sells seashells by the seashore*) on the board or eliciting one or two from the students.

2 Explain that you have identified some sounds that they need to practise. Give a few examples, such as:
l/r – *Laurie's umbrella is red and yellow.*
v/w – *What's a vat of well water worth?*
b/v – *Bev loves borrowing blue envelopes.*

3 Either put students into language groups (if you are teaching a multi-lingual class) or into groups that have similar pronunciation problems.

4 Give each group a pair or set of phonemes to work on.

5 Ask them to use their dictionaries (print or CD-ROM) to find several nouns, verbs, adjectives and adverbs that contain one or both of the sounds in their pairs or sets of words. They will need to consider how the sounds might be spelled.

6 Tell them to make grammatically correct sentences using their words. They don't have to make a lot of sense, they can be absurd. Give them a time limit.

7 Students present their sentences to the other groups. Groups vote on the one(s) they like best.

Variation

A variation on this is to ask the groups to make tongue twisters for each other. Use your own judgement to decide whether this would work for your class.

Note

The main difference between using a book and a CD-ROM to generate word lists of specific phonemes is that a CD-ROM makes it very easy to create lists of words that contain the phoneme in mid- or final position using wildcards.

4.10 Short short stories

Aim	To locate, use and practise a broader range of words containing individual sounds
Focus	Individual sounds
Level	Intermediate and above
Time	35–40 minutes
Preparation	As in activity 4.9, prepare a set of target phonemes for students to work on. If you used the previous activity, you can either extend the number of phonemes you used, or work on new sounds.

Procedure

1 Tell students that they are going to be writing a story using the pre-selected sounds. They can use other words as well, of course, but they should try to use as many of the target sounds as possible.

2 Put students into groups. Give them the target sounds and a (strict) time limit to use their dictionaries to find as many words as they can. Remind them that they will need nouns, verbs, adjectives and adverbs. They can put these into a grid like the one below for initial /r/.

Adjective	Noun	Verb	Adverb
rapid	rabbit	raffle	really
remote	race	raise	roughly
rented	racehorse	read	wrongly
respected	raffle	realize	
rested	room	rearrange	
restful	rope	recall	
retired	rose	recite	
rich	route	record	
rickety	rubbish	recycle	
ripe	rug	rehearse	
roomy	rule	rely	
rude	ruler	remember	
rural	rust		

3 Ask students to use the words they have found to create a story of about ten sentences. Stories need a beginning, a middle and an end. They can be about a thing, a person or a place (and they do not have to be serious).

4 If students need a little more help, brainstorm a few possible characters and start a possible story. For example:

Richard was a retired rabbit that lived in a room in a really remote, rural area. One day he won a racehorse in a raffle. He realized the racehorse could make him rich. Really rich …

5 Set another time limit. Monitor and circulate.

6 When the time is up, ask groups to swap stories. Give them a few minutes to practise reading the stories, checking stress and pronunciation. Then each group reads another group's story aloud to the class.

Note

If you have a monolingual group, or a group whose first languages or pronunciation problems are similar, it is fun to give every group the same set of target sounds, then they can listen to the different words they use and stories they create.

5 Reading and writing activities

The first nine activities in this chapter are primarily reading, decoding activities designed to be used with reference dictionaries such as *CLD* and *CALD*. Activities 5.10–5.12 are writing, encoding activities and work well with production dictionaries like the *Longman Activator* ™.

Production dictionaries are designed to be used to increase productive vocabulary and improve writing. They are an excellent tool for the learner – and the teacher.

They differ significantly from reference dictionaries and are sometimes misunderstood, and are probably underused because of this.

Instead of the familiar reference dictionary sequence of word to meaning (i.e. you see or hear a word, you look it up, you understand the word), production dictionaries work from meaning to word.

Words are grouped around base or key words such as *happy, say* or *walk*. Then, at *walk* there will be a set of signposts directing users to more specific words like *amble, stride, wade, march, shuffle, stomp*, etc.

The important difference between a production dictionary and a thesaurus is that, as well as guiding users to exactly the word they want, production dictionaries have definitions for each word and example sentences.

5.1 Reading: Meaning and context 1

Aim	To use context to guess meaning, then check in dictionary
Focus	Meaning to word (meanings supplied)
Level	Any (the sample text is upper-intermediate)
Time	20 minutes
Preparation	Choose a short text like the one in Box 41, which has several words that may be unfamiliar to your students. Use the dictionary to write short definitions for part B. You may wish to supply line numbers for your text, especially if it is longer than the sample text.

Procedure

1 Ask students to read the text through for general meaning.
2 Ask them to try to find words in the text that mean the same as the words or phrases in part B. Elicit clues that will help (part of speech, meaning of other key words in the sentence, etc.).

3 Ask them to check their answers in the dictionary when they have found a possible match for each word or phrase.

4 Discuss their answers, and their strategies, as a whole class activity.

Box 41

A Read the two paragraphs below for general meaning.

A few years ago I was researching a book about Einstein when I stumbled on a footnote about an obscure Frenchwoman of the early 18th century. Her name was Emilie du Châtelet; according to the note, she had played some role in developing the modern concept of energy, and had acquired a certain notoriety in her day.

It left me intrigued, and hungry to know more. And what I discovered, as I tracked down her letters and books over the next few months, astounded me. Because that footnote had understated her significance entirely. Emilie du Châtelet had played a crucial role in the development of science. What's more, she had had a wild life.

The Guardian

B Find words that mean the same as:

1 discover something by chance (v.) _____
2 not known by many people (adj.) _____
3 being famous for something bad (n.) _____
4 interested (adj.) _____
5 surprised (v.) _____
6 importance (n.) _____

© Cambridge University Press 2007

Answers (Box 41)
1 stumble on   2 obscure   3 notoriety   4 intrigued   5 astounded
6 significance

5.2 Reading: Meaning and context 2

Aim To use context to guess meaning, then check in the dictionary
Focus Word to meaning (meanings not supplied)
Level Any (the sample material is upper-intermediate)
Time 20–30 minutes
Preparation Choose a short text like the one in Box 42, which has several words (underlined) that are likely to be new to your students.

Procedure

1 Ask students to read the text through for general meaning.
2 Ask them to work in pairs and first put a tick next to underlined words they already know, then to try to guess the meanings of the 'new' underlined words. Elicit clues that will help (part of speech, context clues, etc.).
3 Ask them to check their answers in the dictionary.
4 As a whole class activity, discuss their answers, the context clues they used and how successful their guesses were.

Box 42

Read the text below. Use context clues to guess the meanings of the underlined words and phrases. Check your answers in the dictionary.

An ambitious project to safeguard future food supplies began yesterday with the (1) launch of a 'Noah's ark' for the world's most important plants.

'The new Svalbard International Seed Vault will serve as a (2) repository for (3) crucial seeds in the event of a global (4) catastrophe,' said Norway's agriculture minister, Terje Riis-Johansen.

Carved into the (5) permafrost and rock of the remote Svalbard peninsula, it will eventually house 3 million seed samples from every country in the world.

'This facility will provide a practical means to re-establish crops (6) obliterated by major disasters,' said Cary Fowler, the executive secretary of the Global Crop Diversity Trust, which will manage the seed bank. 'But crop diversity is (7) imperilled not just by a (8) cataclysmic event, such as a nuclear war, but also by natural disasters, accidents, mismanagement, and short-sighted budget cuts.'

Agriculture relies on collections of crop species and their wild relatives. Seed banks are (9) vital to the development of new crop varieties and, without them, agriculture would (10) grind to a halt. Samples of the world's agricultural biodiversity, including crops such as wheat, apple and potato, are scattered across 1,400 seed banks around the world.

The Guardian

Word/phrase	Part of speech	Possible meaning
1 launch		
2 repository		
3 crucial		
4 catastrophe		
5 permafrost		
6 obliterated		
7 imperilled		
8 cataclysmic		
9 vital		
10 grind to a halt		

5.3 Confusables

Aim	To encourage students to use the dictionary to check confusable words
Focus	Sentence level writing
Level	Intermediate and above (the sample material is upper-intermediate to advanced)
Time	10–15 minutes
Preparation	Either use the sentences in Box 43 (from *CALD*) or create sentences with pairs of confusable words.

Procedure

1   Write the following gapped sentence on the board:
    She gave me some good _____. (advise / advice)
2   Ask students which word correctly completes the sentence (*advice*).
3   Give students the sentences and put them into groups, with one dictionary per group. Ask them to use their dictionaries to complete the sentences as quickly as possible. The fastest group to complete all the sentences correctly wins.

Box 43

Choose the correct word to complete the sentences.

1 They received a lot of _____ publicity about the changes.
   adverse / averse
2 The radiation leak has had a disastrous _____ on the environment.
   affect / effect
3 Strawberries and cream _____ each other perfectly.
   complement / compliment
4 My computer makes a _____ low buzzing noise.
   continuous / continual
5 These small companies now have their own _____ identity.
   discreet / discrete
6 What do you _____ from her refusal?
   imply / infer
7 That was my _____ reason for moving.
   principal / principle
8 The traffic got slower and slower until it was _____ .
   stationary / stationery
9 Please _____ me to send her an email tomorrow.
   remember / remind
10 When it stopped raining we were _____ to get out in the sun.
   anxious / eager

© Cambridge University Press 2007

Answers (Box 43)

1 adverse   2 effect   3 complement   4 continuous   5 discrete   6 infer
7 principal   8 stationary   9 remind   10 eager

5.4 Formal or informal 1

Aim	To increase student awareness of academic or formal writing style
Focus	Register, dictionary labels
Level	Intermediate and above
Time	20–30 minutes
Preparation	Either use the list in Box 44 (verbs) or create a similar list of formal/informal pairs (see Notes on page 97).

Procedure

1 Explain to students that:
- English is a language that has a lot of synonyms. This is because the language changed and grew as different countries occupied England. For example, the verbs *ask, question*, and *interrogate* all mean roughly the same thing but differ in their level of formality.
- Most academic writing uses the more formal words from French or Latin origins, rather than the Anglo Saxon word.

2 Put students into pairs or groups of three or four with one dictionary per pair or group.

3 Give students the list of words and ask them to work together to match the pairs using the dictionaries. To make this a bit livelier, set it up as a race.

4 Check the answers as a whole class activity.

Box 44

Match the formal words on the left with the more informal words on the right.

Formal	Informal
appear	ask
assist	begin
cease	get
commence	go
consume	help
decrease	keep
demonstrate	keep
depart	live
desire	need
enquire	seem
inform	shorten
obtain	show
preserve	stop
require	tell
reside	use
retain	want

© Cambridge University Press 2007

Notes

1 If you have access to a CD-ROM dictionary, use the search facility and formal/informal label filters to make a list quickly.

2 You may wish to use activity 5.5 to follow up this activity.

Answers (Box 44)

appear – seem   assist – help   cease – stop   commence – begin
consume – use   decrease – shorten   demonstrate – show
depart – go   desire – want   enquire – ask   inform – tell
obtain – get   preserve – keep   require – need   reside – live
retain – keep

5.5 Formal or informal 2

Aim	To practise using the dictionary to check register or style
Focus	Register, dictionary labels
Level	Intermediate and above
Time	10–25 minutes (with the Follow-up)
Preparation	Prepare an informal text, substituting inappropriately formal words for informal words, or use the text in Box 45.

Procedure

1 Ask students to think about the difference between the way they speak or write to friends, and the way they write or speak in more formal situations.

2 Elicit some different types of communication: business letters, phone calls, emails, text messages, etc.

3 Elicit a few differences: use of short forms, slang, etc. in texts and emails; longer sentences, more formal word selection in business letters, etc.

4 Give students the text and tell them to use dictionaries to complete the task.

5 Check the answers as a whole class activity.

Box 45

This email from Sally to her friend sounds far too formal. Replace the words in **bold** with their informal equivalents.

Dear Anna,

How are you feeling? You (1) **appeared** to be a little down yesterday.
I wanted to (2) **enquire** what was wrong before the film (3) **commenced**
but I didn't have a chance.
Then, when it was over, you had already (4) **departed**.
I know that you (5) **require** a cheaper place to (6) **reside**. Is that the problem?
I didn't have a chance to (7) **inform** you that we are looking for a new
roommate to share our place. You would be perfect.
Let me know what you think.

Love,

Sally

© Cambridge University Press 2007

Follow-up
In pairs or groups, students write a formal letter with five or six overly *informal* words, then swap letters with another group.

Note
You may prefer to use an informal → formal text activity first.

Answers (Box 45)
1 seemed   2 ask   3 began/started   4 gone/left   5 need   6 live   7 tell

5.6 Text completion

Aim	To practise choosing the right word
Focus	Sentence level writing
Level	Intermediate and above (the sample material is intermediate)
Time	15–20 minutes (more with the Follow-up)
Preparation	Compile word choice errors from your students' written work or use the sentences in Box 46.

Procedure

1　Ask students to work in pairs or groups of three and use their dictionaries to look up unfamiliar words in the dictionary, then decide which is the best.
2　Go through the first sentence together.
3　Check as a whole class activity.

Box 46

Choose the correct word to complete each sentence.

1　Their nearest neighbours live two miles away. They live in a/an _____ spot.
　　a urban　　b remote　　c regional

2　It's a _____ you can't come to the party.
　　a shame　　b humiliation　　c disgrace

3　It is the _____ building in the city.
　　a highest　　b tallest　　c loftiest

4　They had their fortunes told by a woman who _____ people's futures.
　　a predicts　　b forecasts　　c forewarns

5　It was a cloudy day, which made everyone feel a little _____ .
　　a shady　　b overcast　　c gloomy

6　He got _____ with the wrong sort of people.
　　a involved　　b mixed　　c intermingled

7　The president's resignation threw the country into _____ .
　　a trouble　　b disturbance　　c turmoil

8　Some people in Britain grow vegetables and flowers on their _____ .
　　a meadows　　b allotments　　c pastures

9　The food was good and the prices are really quite _____ .
　　a realistic　　b reasonable　　c reassuring

10　Are there any _____ available for the evening performance?
　　a places　　b spaces　　c seats

© Cambridge University Press 2007

Follow-up

Ask students to write sentences using the other two words in each item.

Answers (Box 46)
1b, 2a, 3b, 4a, 5c, 6a, 7c, 8b, 9b, 10c

5.7 Academic writing: Discourse markers

Aim	To extend academic vocabulary and organization skills
Focus	Signalling words
Level	Upper-intermediate–Advanced
Time	25–35 minutes
Preparation	Either use the list in Box 47 or prepare a list of signalling words and phrases of various categories.

Procedure

1 Explain that, in academic writing, it is important to show how the ideas (and the parts of a paragraph) are connected. These words or phrases are called *discourse markers*: they signal a writer's intention and make the connections clear to the reader.
2 Put the main headings on the board:
   Order   Comparison   Contrast   Cause/effect   Support   Generalization
3 Elicit an example for each heading. If necessary, prompt students with a few low level words or phrases like *but, so, first*, etc. and ask them to put them under the correct heading. (It doesn't matter if students give one or two from the list. It is quite a long list.)
4 Give students the list and ask them to work in pairs or small groups.
5 Check as a whole class activity.

Box 47

A Use a dictionary to put the signalling words and phrases below into
the correct groups.

Order	Comparison	Contrast	Cause/effect	Support	Generalization

accordingly
as a result
as a rule
consequently
even so
eventually
finally

for example
for instance
for the most part
in comparison
in contrast
in spite of
in the same way

lastly
on the whole
similarly
such as
whereas

B Using the dictionary entries, choose the correct word or phrase.

1 Firstly … Secondly … Thirdly … *Eventually / Finally* …
2 The research was flawed. As a *rule / result*, the study was never published.
3 Possible solutions, *such as / whereas* stricter laws, were considered.
4 *Although / In spite of* the plan was costly, it was the one selected.

© Cambridge University Press 2007

Follow-up
Create an exercise with your students' common errors from the list you used
in A, using the sentences in B as a model.

Note
Very common, lower level items such as *but, so, first*, etc. should already be
within students' control at this stage.

Answers (Box 47)

A

Order	Comparison	Contrast	Cause/effect	Support	Generalization
eventually	in comparison	even so	accordingly	for example	as a rule
finally	in the same way	in contrast	as a result	for instance	for the most part
lastly	similarly	in spite of	consequently	such as	on the whole
		whereas			

B   1 Finally   2 result   3 such as   4 Although

5.8 Punctuation

Aim To use the dictionary study pages to punctuate text
Focus Paragraph level writing
Level Lower-intermediate and above (the sample text is upper-intermediate)
Time 20 minutes
Preparation Collect a few punctuation mistakes that your students have made recently. Also choose a text that is appropriate for your students and remove the punctuation or use the sample text in Box 48. Put the punctuated text on an OHP so you can check it with the class after they have done the task. Also check the study pages in your dictionary. (The Punctuation study pages in *CALD* are on Centre 36–7.)

Procedure

1   Write a few of your students' incorrectly punctuated sentences on the board.
2   Ask students to work in pairs, using the relevant study pages in the dictionary to correct the sentences.
3   Give students the unpunctuated text to punctuate in pairs.
4   Check on an OHP as a whole class activity, eliciting the punctuation line by line.

Box 48

Use the study pages in the dictionary and punctuate this text.

a drug developed to treat allergies has been identified by us researchers as a potential cure for malaria tests in mice show that the antihistamine astemizole also kills the malaria parasite it is already licensed for use in people so it could be developed for use as a malaria drug in about 12 months and because it is no longer under patent it will be possible to manufacture it at rock-bottom prices the breakthrough has excited researchers because of the cost of developing other anti-malarial treatments time and money are major roadblocks when it comes to developing new drugs for neglected diseases like malaria said david sullivan at the johns hopkins bloomberg school of public health in baltimore maryland who led the team.

The Guardian

© Cambridge University Press 2007

Punctuated text

Some variation is possible
A drug developed to treat allergies has been identified by US researchers as a potential cure for malaria. Tests in mice show that the antihistamine astemizole also kills the malaria parasite. It is already licensed for use in people, so it could be developed for use as a malaria drug in about 12 months. And because it is no longer under patent, it will be possible to manufacture it at rock-bottom prices.

The breakthrough has excited researchers because of the cost of developing other anti-malarial treatments. 'Time and money are major roadblocks when it comes to developing new drugs for neglected diseases like malaria,' said David Sullivan at the Johns Hopkins Bloomberg School of Public Health in Baltimore, Maryland, who led the team.

5.9 Mini-stories

Aim	To have fun using example sentences to write a story
Focus	Cohesion in extended writing (and fun)
Level	Intermediate and above
Time	30–40 minutes
Preparation	Select several random example sentences from the dictionary or use the ones below (from *CALD*).

Procedure

1   Ask students to work in pairs or groups of three and use the example sentences to write a mini-story (with a beginning, a middle and an end) that makes sense.
2   An additional challenge is to use as many of the example sentences as possible.
3   Ask students to swap stories and read out another group's story.

Example sentences

Do you think Tim's avoiding me? I haven't seen him all day.
He concocted a story about working late at the office.
He was the very worst sort of slimy salesman.
Incredibly, no one was hurt in the accident.
The highs and lows of life tend to average out in the end.

Follow-up
Students select a set of example sentences to challenge other pairs or groups.

5.10 The dice game

Aim	To introduce students to production dictionaries
Focus	Building vocabulary (here the focus is on verbs)
Level	Intermediate and above
Time	45 minutes
Preparation	You will need production dictionaries and a dice for this game.

Procedure

1   Explain to the students that a production dictionary is like a very powerful thesaurus because it not only gives you a list of near-synonyms, but also has definitions and example sentences.

2   Tell them that they are going to rewrite a rather boring story:
A famous person walked up to another famous person and said, '_____.'
The (second person) laughed and said, '_____.'

3   Put the students into groups of four to six. Ask each group to appoint a scribe.
Tell students that they are going to make numbered lists and you will throw the dice. Tell them to make only one list (per group) at a time. These are the instructions:

- First, make a list of six different **famous people**. Number them. *(At this point, you throw the dice. If, for example, a 4 comes up, the person at number 4 on each list is the person that group's story is going to be about.)*
- Now use the dictionary to make a list of six different words for *walk*. Number them. *(You throw the dice. If, for example, a 3 comes up, the word at number 3 on each list is the word they will use in their story.)*
- Go back to the list of famous people and add one more to replace the person you began the story with. Number them. *(You throw the dice.)*
- Now use the dictionary to make a list of six different words for *said*. Number them. *(You throw the dice.)*
- Think of something that this person could have said.
- Now use the dictionary to make a list of six words for *laugh*. Number them. *(You throw the dice.)*
- Think of something the second person could reply.

4   Give students time to go through their stories and check the spelling and grammar (especially the tenses) of the new words. Then ask them to read out their 'mini-stories'. With early finishers, suggest that they add details that will make their story funnier, more interesting or exciting.

Notes

1   The reason for starting with a list of famous people is to accustom the students to the format of the game before they start accessing the dictionary.
2   This is a very effective activity. It shows students how to get the most out of a production dictionary (monolingual or bilingual) and can be lots of fun. See also 8.2 Production dictionaries.
3   Bilingual dictionaries should only be used for this activity with monolingual classes.

5.11 Extreme dialogue writing

Aim	To build productive vocabulary
Focus	Adjectives
Level	Intermediate and above
Time	20–30 minutes
Preparation	Prepare a dialogue or use the holiday dialogue in Box 49.

Procedure

1   Put a scale on the board:

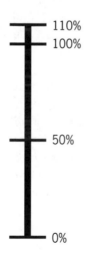

2   Then write *uneasy, petrified* and *scared* below the scale. Ask students where on the scale the words should go.
3   Ask students to work in pairs or groups and use their dictionaries to complete the dialogue with the '110% version' of the words underlined in the dialogue.

4 Check answers together. (You could discuss the intensifiers *absolutely*, *completely*, etc. Some dictionaries have a usage note explaining that extreme adjectives don't usually take intensifiers like *very*.)

5 Ask groups to write similar gapped dialogues to swap with other groups.

Box 49

Extreme holiday

Use your dictionary to complete the dialogue with extreme adjectives.

A: Tell us about your holiday.
B: Well, when we got there, the first thing we wanted to do was get something to eat.
A: Were you <u>hungry</u>?
B: Hungry? We were _____ !
A: Was the food <u>good</u>?
B: Good? It was _____ ! But the hotel room wasn't as tidy as it should have been.
A: Was it <u>dirty</u>?
B: Dirty? It was _____ ! But they cleaned it up right away. They were so helpful.
A: Oh, so the people were <u>nice</u>?
B: Nice? They were _____ !
A: What was the weather like? Was it <u>hot</u>?
B: Hot? It was absolutely _____ most of the time! But it rained the one day we went into town.
A: Did you get <u>wet</u>?
B: Wet? We were completely _____ !
A: But the beach was <u>beautiful</u>, wasn't it?
B: Yes, it was absolutely _____ ! I can't wait to get back there!
A: You're going back <u>soon</u>?
B: Soon? We're going back _____ !

© Cambridge University Press 2007

Possible answers (Box 49)
hungry – starving   good – fantastic   dirty – filthy   nice – charming /
terrific   hot – boiling / sweltering   wet – soaked / drenched   beautiful
– gorgeous / fabulous   soon – right away / as soon as possible

5.12 Fairy story

Aim	To increase productive vocabulary
Focus	Adjectives
Level	Intermediate and above
Time	20–30 minutes
Preparation	Write a short skeleton story for students to embellish or use the one in Box 50.

Procedure

1   Put *fairy story* (or the name of a fairy story your students are likely to be familiar with) on the board.
2   Brainstorm the characters in fairy stories (monsters, beautiful princesses, handsome princes, frogs, evil stepmothers, etc.), the places (castles, magic forests, etc.) and plots.
3   Ask them how fairy stories start (*Once upon a time . . .*).
4   Ask them to work in groups and use their dictionaries to replace the underlined words with more interesting words, then develop the story, introduce more characters and write an ending. Set a time limit.
5   Monitor, check and encourage.
6   When students have finished, ask them to swap stories and read them aloud to the whole class.

Box 50

Use your dictionary to replace the <u>underlined</u> words with more interesting words. Then develop the story, introduce more characters and write an ending.

Once upon a time, in a <u>small</u> pond <u>far</u> away, there lived a <u>beautiful</u> frog. The frog was very lonely and <u>wanted</u> to go somewhere but didn't know where to go.
Then, one day a <u>big</u> circus camped near the pond.
The frog was <u>happy</u>! What <u>good</u> luck!
There were lots of <u>unusual</u> creatures the frog had never seen before.

© Cambridge University Press 2007

Note
Other genres of story can be used as well, e.g. folk tales, jokes, tall stories, ghost stories, urban myths, etc.

These are short activities that can be used as lead-ins or fillers when there is an extra five minutes. They help your students become familiar with the multiple uses of different kinds of dictionary.

6.1 Picture this! Memory game

Aim	To lead in to an activity, activate vocabulary on a given topic and encourage use of picture pages in dictionaries
Focus	Topic vocabulary
Level	Any (the sample material is intermediate)
Time	5–10 minutes (more with the Follow-up)
Preparation	Locate an appropriate composite page or screen with a number of items.

Procedure

1 Choose a page or screen from the picture section of a dictionary (print or CD-ROM) which complements the lesson you are leading into. For example, if you are working on health and fitness, you might use the composite picture on page Centre 10 in *CALD* – Sports 1.

football (UK) soccer (US)

American football (UK) football (US)

tennis

flag

caddie

club

golf — hole

basketball

cricket

hockey (UK) field hockey (US)

2 Tell students you are going to see how good their memories are today.
3 Give them a suitably challenging time limit to study the picture and memorize as many sports as they can, for example 30–45 seconds. Tell them to open their books at page Centre 10.
4 After the time limit, tell them to close their books and write down as many of the sports as they can remember. (This can be done as a solo, pair or group activity.)
5 Check together as a whole class activity.

Follow-up

If you have time and want to extend the activity, create a simple ranking exercise similar to the one below. Ask students to work in groups and decide whether skill, stamina or strength is most important in each of these sports. (Pre-teach or check understanding of *skill, stamina* and *strength*.)

Sport	Skill	Stamina	Strength
cricket			
football			
rock climbing			
rugby			
skiing			
surfing			
swimming			
tennis			

Note

If you are using the picture section from a dictionary on CD-ROM on one central computer, you can easily control the amount of time the pictures are visible as well as how long the text is visible.

6.2 Spelling

Aim	To practise correcting spelling mistakes
Focus	Student spelling errors
Level	Pre-intermediate and above (the sample material is upper-intermediate)
Time	5–10 minutes
Preparation	Compile spelling errors from your students' written work or use the words in Box 51.

Procedure

1 Ask students to work in pairs or groups of three and use their dictionaries to look up unfamiliar words in the dictionary, and correct them as quickly as they can.
2 Make it into a race or set a time limit.
3 Check as a whole class activity.

Box 51

Look up the words in the dictionary and complete the table.

Word	Correct or incorrect?	Corrected spelling
alright		
cemetary		
definately		
desparate		
developement		
exceed		
judgement		
liquify		
ocassion		
reccommend		
recieve		
seperate		
sieze		

© Cambridge University Press 2007

6.3 Topic brainstorm

Aim	To lead in to a reading, listening or writing task; to establish what active vocabulary students have in a given topic area
Focus	Any topic area
Level	Any
Time	5 minutes
Preparation	Locate a picture in your dictionary that will generate some vocabulary in the topic area you want to introduce.

Procedure

1 Show the visual you have chosen.
2 Either as a whole class activity or as a pairwork activity, ask students to write down as many related words as possible in two minutes, then check them in the dictionary.
3 Elicit the words and put them on the board.

Variation

Do this with bilingual dictionaries: brainstorm topic-related words in the L1, then students check their translations in the bilingual dictionary.

6.4 Senses brainstorm

Aim	Vocabulary building
Focus	Multi-sense (polysemous) words
Level	Intermediate and above
Time	5–10 minutes
Preparation	Select several polysemous words you would like to extend or use words from the list below.

Procedure

1 Ask students to work in pairs or groups.
2 Give each pair or group one or two words to work on.
3 Ask them to use their dictionaries to find as many senses of each word as possible.
4 Then take two different meanings and put them into one sentence, e.g.
   Don't batter the batter, you'll ruin it!
   Please page all the guests on page 5.
   Tap the tap with a hammer.
5 Ask them to present their words and sentences to the rest of the class.

batter	race
line	season
mind	table
mint	tack
page	tap

6.5 Idioms brainstorm

Aim	Vocabulary building; lead in to an idioms lesson
Focus	Idioms
Level	Intermediate and above
Time	10 minutes
Preparation	Choose an idiom-rich topic such as *family, feelings, health, memory,* etc. or idiom-rich keywords such as *colours, animals,* etc. Check that your examples (see below) are in the dictionary your students are using.

Procedure

1 Put your topic or keywords on the board.

2 Add one idiom yourself, then ask students to brainstorm all the related idioms (in English) they can think of. For example:

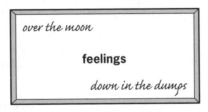

3 Ask them to locate the idioms in the dictionary. (Most dictionaries put idioms entries at the first main content word in the phrase, e.g. *over the moon* is defined at *moon.*)

4 Ask them to think of more idioms (in their language) related to the topic. Are these the same or similar to idioms in English?

5 Ask them to check their L1 idioms in the dictionary, then report back to the class.

6.6 Vocabulary box

Aim	Vocabulary building
Focus	Recycling vocabulary
Level	Pre-intermediate and above
Time	1–2 minutes, ongoing
Preparation	If you teach in the same classroom every lesson, put a shoebox on a desk or pin a folder or large envelope to the wall. If not, make whatever you use easily portable.

Procedure

1   When new items of vocabulary are learned, ask a student to write the word or phrase on a piece of card or paper, use their dictionaries to mark the stress and write a short definition of the word on the back of the card.

2   Put the cards into the box/file/envelope and use them for quick spelling quizzes or vocabulary revision, or peer/self-testing when you (or the students) have a few minutes.

6.7 Describe and draw

Aim	Vocabulary consolidation: appearance
Focus	Face and hair vocabulary
Level	Elementary / Picture dictionaries
Time	5 minutes
Preparation	Make sure you have enough picture dictionaries.

Procedure

1   Ask students to work in pairs with one copy of the picture dictionary per pair.

2   Ask one student (A) to select one of the people on the page and describe him/her to their partner (B) who quickly draws it.

3   Student B then looks at the page and guesses which person Student A was describing.

4   Students swap roles.

Note

This can also be used for other picture pages such as types of *houses, rooms, landscapes*, etc.

6.8 DIY pre-teaching

Aim	To prepare for a reading or listening text
Focus	Preparing students for a reading or listening text
Level	Pre-intermediate and above
Time	5–10 minutes
Preparation	Prepare a list of five to ten words you want to pre-teach before a reading or listening text. Optionally, prepare a simple matching activity for the check phase.

Procedure

1 Show students the list of words.
2 Give them two minutes to look up the meanings of as many of the words as possible.
3 Check as a whole class activity.
   If you are using the matching activity: put it on the board or an OHT, give students some time in pairs or small groups to decide which meanings go with each word, then elicit the matches.

6.9 Associations

Aim	To practise using the dictionary and understanding definitions
Focus	Dictionary skills
Level	Intermediate and above
Time	2–3 minutes

Procedure

1 Ask one student to open the dictionary and put his/her finger on a word at random.
2 Ask the student to read the word and the definition to the class.
3 Write the word on the board.
4 Ask another student to repeat the exercise, and write that word on the board.
5 Ask students to use both words in a single sentence.

6.10 Hairy headlines

Aim	To have fun looking up polysemous (multi-sense) items
Focus	Polysemous words
Level	Upper-intermediate and above
Time	5–10 minutes (or longer if you want)
Preparation	Locate a few ambiguous headlines or use the ones on page 116.

Procedure

1 Put one of the headlines on the board and ask students to work in pairs using their dictionaries to find out why it is funny.
2 Give each pair or group a headline to work on.
3 Ask students to explain the two meanings of each headline. (If your class is monolingual, ask them to translate the headlines in the two possible interpretations.)

Drunk gets nine months in violin case

Stolen painting found by tree

Red tape holds up bridge

Grandmother of eight makes hole in one

Milk drinkers are turning to powder

Police discover crack in Australia

Bank of China floats in Shanghai

People turn to beans

6.11 Categories

Aim	To practise skimming dictionary pages
Focus	Skimming
Level	Pre-intermediate
Time	5–10 minutes
Preparation	Prepare three or four categories of words you want to present.

Procedure

1 Give students a grid like the one below. (Use any categories you would like to work on.)
2 Set a time limit or make this a race.
3 Call out a letter at random.
4 Students use their dictionaries (monolingual or bilingual) to write as many words as they can beginning with that letter for each category.

Food	Clothing	Parts of the body	Animals

6.12 Name cards

Aim	Vocabulary building
Focus	Adjectives
Age	Teenagers
Level	Intermediate
Time	10–15 minutes
Preparation	You will need rectangular sheets of card, one for each student.

Procedure

1 Give each student a sheet of card.
2 Ask them to fold it in half.
3 Ask them to write the name of a friend or relative (preferably a short name) vertically down the left side of the card.

4 Ask them to use their dictionaries to find adjectives (or intensifiers + adjectives – see example) beginning with each letter of the name.

Note

This is fun for holidays, birthdays, name days, etc.

7 CD-ROM and electronic dictionary activities

When publishers began putting multimedia dictionaries on CD-ROMs, it revolutionized dictionaries. Suddenly, all sorts of things were possible: students could hear pronunciations, not just read them; pictures and video could be used to illustrate meaning and context; powerful links and cross-references could be created. But the biggest difference was that there was space. A great deal of text – about the equivalent of 60 advanced-level print dictionaries – could be included on a CD-ROM.

Sound, video, text and functionality (search engines, hot-links, etc.) all take up space, though. And dictionaries on CD-ROM vary in terms of features. In some cases, publishers have decided to include more functionality and less text, or have opted for big banks of examples and no video.

However, all the main ELT publishers' dictionaries have these things in common:

- The definitions are hot-linked – each word in a definition can be clicked on and the user will be taken to a definition of that word.
- There is pronunciation of all the headwords, often in both American and British English.
- There is a search facility, although these vary in functionality.
- There are interactive activities or exercises.
- There are pictures, usually labelled and linked to definitions.

The CD-ROM activities in this chapter are designed to work on any of the main ELT publishers' dictionaries.

CD-ROM activities

7.1 Exploring your dictionary

Aim	To explore the CD-ROM and become familiar with the features
Focus	General introduction to using the dictionary
Level	Lower-intermediate and above
Time	20 minutes
Preparation	Install the CD-ROM and familiarize yourself with the features you will be showing. This activity will work on a single stand-alone computer with or without a projector, although a projector is much better because it is easier for the students to see what is happening on screen.

Procedure

1 Ask students how CD-ROM dictionaries differ from print dictionaries. They may or may not know about the features as described on page 119.

2 Start by typing in a word in the lookup window. Use an item of vocabulary from a topic area you are working on. For example, *environment*. Make a deliberate spelling error toward the end of the word to demonstrate that you can still find the word, even if the spelling is not completely accurate. This will take you to *environment* in *CALD*. The next entry is *the environment*.

3 Click on the pronunciation symbol to hear how the word is pronounced, and the various buttons that are active for that word. (In *CALD* these are the 'word building', 'collocations' and 'smart thesaurus' buttons.) Double-click on one of the longer words in the definition to show how the word is hot-linked. The definition for that word will appear.

4 Draw students' attention to the example sentences.

5 Show them the print, copy and help buttons.

6 Look at the exercises and activities. If you have time, do one together.

7 Go through the other databases and show them the various features in each. (For example, in the *CALD* pictures database, the first composite picture to appear is 'animals'. If you are using *CALD*, click on the lion to show that *mane* is also labelled, or the camel to show that *hump* is labelled.)

8 Go to the search facility. (In *CALD*, this is 'Advanced search'.) Show students how the various filters work.

Follow-up

If you have time, go on to do one of the other activities in this unit.

7.2 Idioms

Aim	To build idiomatic vocabulary, to increase awareness of idioms in both formal and informal English; to practise using the search facility to build vocabulary
Focus	Idioms
Level	Upper-intermediate and above
Time	15–20 minutes
Preparation	Check the search and filter facility on the dictionary that you are using.

Procedure

1 Ask students what an idiom is. Elicit any that you may have discussed before. Ask them whether idioms are formal or informal. (You can either tell them that they are not just informal or wait and show them in the next stage of the lesson.)

2 Show students how to access the search facility and how to use the filters. If you are using *CALD*, select 'idioms' in the category field, 'formal' in the usage field, and 'feelings' in the topic field (or the topic you have chosen – making sure to check that you will have enough hits with the 'formal' filter on). You will see this screen:

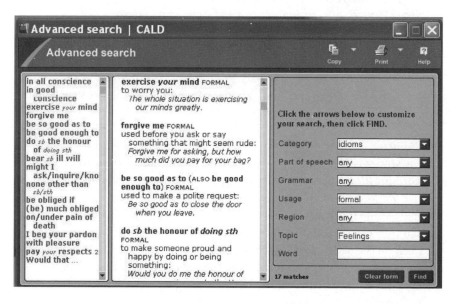

Now take the 'formal' filter off. There will be many more idioms but it is useful to show students that idioms occur in all sorts of contexts.

3   Either choose topic areas that you have been working on or ask students to choose one. In small groups, they should work on their topic area and find four to six idioms related to that area. They need to find the meanings, how they are used in a sentence and whether they are formal or informal.
They can either write their results on paper or on screen if there are presentation facilities available.
Circulate and monitor. Check that they have chosen useful idioms, not the 'raining cats and dogs' colourful but infrequent sort.

4   Students present their idioms. Ask them to tell the class what their idioms are, what they mean and how to use them in a sentence.

Follow-up
You may want to play an idioms bingo game, using items selected from each group. (See 2.8 Word building 2 for the procedure.)

7.3   British and American English

Aim	To increase awareness of British/American vocabulary; to introduce searches using regional labels
Focus	Lexical differences in British and American English
Level	Intermediate and above
Time	15–20 minutes
Preparation	Either prepare a list of differences in British and American English or use the one in Box 52. (This activity uses the terminology used in *CALD*. The search facility and the terminology will vary depending on which dictionary you are using.)

Procedure
1   Ask students what an *elevator* is. (Elicit that it is the American English word for *lift*.) Ask them if they know of any other British/American pairs. (They may know *tap/faucet, underground/subway*, etc.)
2   Show students how to access the search facility on the dictionary. Explain that they can set different filters to refine their searches.
3   Click on the 'Advanced search' button.
4   Select the category 'headwords' and the region 'British English only'. Type *flat* in the word window. The following screen will appear:

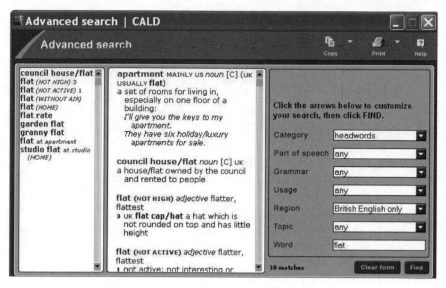

5 Give out, or email, the students the word list.
6 Explain that they will need to switch back and forth between American and British English in order to find all the matches.

Box 52

Match the British English words on the left with their American English equivalents on the right.

British English	American English
flat	sidewalk
mark	review
note	homely
pavement	grade
petrol	gas
plaster	bill
pram	band-aid
revise	bachelor party
stag night	baby buggy
ugly	apartment

© Cambridge University Press 2007

Follow-up
Give students film titles to 'translate' from British English to American English or vice versa, e.g. *The Apartment, Summer Holiday, My Beautiful Launderette, The Lion, the Witch and the Wardrobe, Platoon, High School.*

Answers (Box 52)
flat – apartment   mark – grade   note – bill   pavement – sidewalk
petrol – gas   plaster – band-aid   pram – baby buggy   revise – review
stag night – bachelor party   ugly – homely

7.4 Pictures

Aim	To activate and/or extend vocabulary on a given topic and encourage use of the picture screens
Focus	Topic vocabulary
Level	Any
Time	15 minutes
Preparation	Choose a screen from the picture database (the example is from *CALD*).

toaster

Procedure

1 Put students into pairs or small groups, each with access to the dictionary on screen. Tell them they are going to look at a picture screen and try to write down as many words as they can. Then they are going to find related items as quickly as possible. **They will need to click on each item and read its definition to find a related word.**

2 The first group to list all the items or activities pictured and a related word for each wins.

3 For example, in the Kitchen equipment and cooking screen shown, there are 21 items pictured: 12 nouns and nine verbs. They need to write down not only the item given, e.g. *fry* (verb) but also the piece of equipment used for that action, *frying pan*. Or, in the case of the noun being given, e.g. *scale*, they should also write *weigh*. (This screen has both the noun and verb for *grate* and *grater*.)

Noun	Verb
kettle	boil

4 Direct students to the screen you have chosen and set a time limit.

5 Check together as a whole class activity.

7.5 Lexical chains 1

Aim	To identify lexical chains in a text and use the CD-ROM to produce chains
Focus	Writing
Level	Intermediate and above
Time	30–40 minutes
Preparation	Select a text with a strong lexical chain or use the one in Box 53. Think of several topics you have covered, or are planning to cover, to assign to students in step 3.

Procedure

1 Put the text topic on the board and brainstorm a few words that might occur in the text. For example:

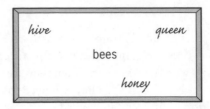

2 Give students the text and ask them to underline other words from the lexical chain and any other strong lexical chains (*death* in this text).

3 Ask students to work in groups. Give each group a topic and ask them to use the search facility to brainstorm a lexical chain for that topic, then write a text incorporating the chain.

4 Monitor and check.

5 Ask groups to swap texts and repeat step 2 above with the new text.

Box 53

Underline words from the lexical chain and any other strong lexical chains.

Undertakers are not as rare in the bee world as biologists once thought. Though only 5 to 10 per cent of bees make a career of removing corpses from the hive, about 25 per cent have a go at one time or another, say scientists in Connecticut.

Bees change occupations throughout their adult life. Young adults attend to the queen and clean the hive. In old age, they go out and forage. But middle-aged bees take up a wide variety of jobs including accepting food from foragers, guarding the hive, working with wax and, in some cases, disposing of dead bodies.

Almost all middle-aged bees do some wax work and accept food into the hive, but few become dedicated undertakers. Undertaker bees have the job of lugging a dead hive-mate towards the exit, then flying the carcass about 100 metres away before jettisoning it.

New Scientist

© Cambridge University Press 2007

7.6 Lexical chains 2

Aim	To identify lexical chains and metaphor in a song
Focus	Writing
Level	Intermediate and above
Time	30–40 minutes
Preparation	Ask students to bring in the lyrics of a song they like which has a lexical chain or use the song in Box 54.

Procedure

1 Put the song title (or topic) on the board and brainstorm a few words that might occur in the text. For example:

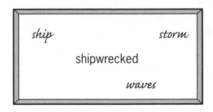

2 Give students the text and ask them to underline other words from the lexical chain (*sea, sailing*) and words that describe those words (such as *cruel, heavy*).

3 Elicit reasons why the songwriter chose the lyrics (and metaphor) and what he/she wanted to convey (the importance of taking risks in life, rising to challenges?).

4 Ask students to work in groups. Ask each group to choose a theme (independence, courage, love, risk, discovery, etc.) and to consider possible metaphors for the theme, then use the search facility on the CD-ROM to create a lexical chain based on the metaphor with possible collocations.

5 Ask students to write a song or poem incorporating the chain.

6 Monitor and check.

7 Give students time to read each other's songs or poems.

Box 54

Shipwrecked

May be heavy
May be cruel
Be the hammer
Your own tool

Every new morning
Belongs to me
Leave the broken glass rain
And the crippling stains
And find a brand new Galilee.
We all keep making those same old yesterdays
We all keep making those same old yesterdays.

Better to be shipwrecked, better to be shipwrecked
Better to be shipwrecked, than never sail at all.

Where everything is crazy
The feeders feed
Every friction craves an addiction
Every voyeur holds the key

There'll be no sailing
In this company
But I will sail to where safety failed
Far into the unknown sea.

We all keep making those same old yesterdays
We all keep making those same old yesterdays.

Better to be shipwrecked, better to be shipwrecked
Better to be shipwrecked, than never sail at all.

We all keep making those same old yesterdays
We all keep making those same old yesterdays.

Better to be shipwrecked, better to be shipwrecked
Better to be shipwrecked, than never sail at all.

Derrin Nauendorf

7.7 Haiku

Aim	To practise using the CD-ROM search facility to write short poems
Focus	Writing poetry using the dictionary
Level	Intermediate and above
Time	30–40 minutes
Preparation	Prepare examples of Haiku or use the poems below.

Procedure

1 Explain what Haiku is:
   - A poem of 17 syllables in three groups: 5–7–5.
   - The first or second line ends in a colon or a dash, 'splitting' the poem into two parts.
   - It is a poetic snapshot.
   - It often contains a reference to nature. This may be something that is associated with the seasons, for example a lamb in spring, mosquitoes in the summer, leaves turning in the autumn, frost in the winter.

2 Give a few examples. (It is best if the students can hear as well as see them.)

> A giant firefly:
> that way, this way, that way, this –
> and it passes by.
> > **Issa** (1762–1826)

> First autumn morning:
> the mirror I stare into
> shows my father's face.
> > **Murakami, Kijo** (1865–1938)

3 As a whole class activity, brainstorm ideas using the dictionary. If you are using the *CALD* or *CLD* CD-ROM, look up *nature*, then click on 'smart thesaurus' for a list of 'season' words to generate ideas.

4 In groups, students choose a season and write a poem together. Remind them that the 5–7–5 syllable pattern and split are important so they need to check the number of syllables of each word.

5 Monitor and check.

6 Groups read out their Haiku.

Note

If you have display space, putting the finished poems on the wall is motivating.

Electronic and online dictionary activities

7.8 Concordances and corpora

Aim	To introduce concordancing and corpora
Focus	Partial synonyms and their collocations
Level	Intermediate and above
Time	30 minutes
Preparation	Check the concordancer website you intend to use; content and functionality change.

Procedure

1 Explain that language corpora are very large databases of language that are searchable in a number of ways. The language in a corpus may be written, spoken or both.

2 Tell the students that they will be using a corpus to find out more about the collocations (words that are frequently used with each other) and usage of groups of words that are similar, but not the same.

3 Put the following on the board:
   Partial synonyms – How are these the same? How are they different?
   • high / tall
   • propose / suggest
   • refuse / decline / reject / turn down

4 Using an online corpus with a simple concordancer (see page 146 for addresses), first type in *high* and show the results:

```
ld be optimistic in nature and have high aspirations."
a trough over the northern Rockies, high pressure in the northwest bringing
s that are thriving: foreign trade, high technology, professional services
        Volume returned to its recent high levels after Monday's abbreviated
sons, which I can do by taking very high energy protons and making them col
meownership, from discrimination to high closing costs.
                    "It's half as high on an average daily basis, as in N
```

© Cambridge International Corpus

5 Discuss the words to the right of *high*. Draw students' attention to collocates such as (in the example above) *pressure, levels, costs*, etc. Note some of the important and high frequency collocates on the board.

6 Type in *tall* and follow the same steps.

```
feet wide, and 3 feet deep, with a tall, wide doorway.
t she pulled her gaze away from the tall figure clad in blue trousers and bl
Theodora 's mind flashed back to the tall washed-out figure of Mrs Gray and h
                        <$1>It is this tall building with no windows.
               One-woman man, tall, dark, handsome, rich, generous, k
            <$M>She's about as tall as I am.
```

© Cambridge International Corpus

7 If you have access to multiple computers, ask students to continue the activity in pairs or groups of three and note down differences and similarities. If you do not, continue as a whole class activity.

Notes

1 Some online sites allow multiple concordances, which are ideal for this activity.
Always check (and recheck) Internet sites when planning online sessions. Addresses, content and access change.

2 This activity can also be used to distinguish between commonly confused words, too, like *lie* and *lay*, or *affect* and *effect*. It can also be used to discover common collocations, e.g. Is it *different from/than/to*? Does *enjoy* take *-ing* or the infinitive? etc.

I am grateful to Phil Schofield at Essex University, who originally gave me the idea for this activity.

7.9 Word and phrase origins

Aim	To increase student interest in language
Focus	Idioms
Level	Intermediate and above
Time	5–10 minutes per idiom; it can be used as an ongoing project
Preparation	Prepare a list of idioms you would like students to research, perhaps in a topic area, or use idioms in Box 55. (All the idioms on this list have fairly clear etymologies.) Check websites and search engines and the example idiom search you plan to do as a demonstration.

Procedure

This can be done as a whole class activity with one classroom computer, but it works best in a lab with two or three students to a computer.

1 First do a search on one of the idioms together. You can either use one of the online etymology dictionaries listed on page 146 or a search engine.

Dictionary Activities

2 If you are using a search engine, type in *phrase origin* and the idiom you are looking up.
3 Give each pair or group three or four idioms to research.
4 Circulate and monitor.
5 Ask students to present their idioms and origins.

Box 55

Idiom	Meaning	Origin
a chip off the old block		
a needle in a haystack		
beat about/around the bush		
bring home the bacon		
fly by the seat of your pants		
get out of bed on the wrong side		
have a chip on one's shoulder		
once in a blue moon		
put my two cents in		
put your cards on the table		
take the gloves off		
throw in the towel		
to drown your sorrows		
under the weather		
up to scratch		
wear your heart on your sleeve		
wet behind the ears		

© Cambridge University Press 2007

Note
There are some etymology sites that generate big discussions on word origin.
They can be a bit long-winded but are sometimes very interesting.

8　Specialized dictionaries

There are a number of specialized dictionaries available that target different learner types and needs. These include dictionaries of idioms, or phrasal verbs, as well as bilingual dictionaries and picture dictionaries.

Bilingual dictionaries

In addition to the two activities in this section, many of the activities found elsewhere in the book, targeted at higher levels and using monolingual dictionaries, are accessible to lower levels using bilingual dictionaries.

The following activities can all be adapted for bilingual dictionaries: 2.1 Learner training: Recording vocabulary, 2.6 Collocations 3: Adjective + noun dominoes, 4.6 Odd one out, 6.3 Topic brainstorm.

8.1　Word maze

Aim	Vocabulary building
Focus	Polysemous (multi-sense) words and translations
Level	Pre-intermediate and above
Time	10–15 minutes (more with the Follow-up)
Preparation	Prepare a few polysemous English words or use words from the list below.

Procedure

1　Ask students to work in groups.
2　Give students a richly polysemous word to begin with, for example, *print, branch, spring, date, head*, etc.
3　They need to look that word up in the English → L1 section of a bilingual dictionary (print or handheld). They choose one of the meanings (translated) and look that word up in the L1 → English section. (See the English → Spanish example mazes which follow.)
4　They then choose one of the meanings (translated) there to look up in the English → L1 section, and so on.
5　The group who can make the longest maze wins.

Examples of mazes

1 **spring** – [fuente] – origin – [causa] – motive – [motor] – engine – [maquina] – scheme – [proyecto] – idea – [opinion] – view – [vista] – sight – [spectaculo]
2 **print** – [marca] – mark – [señal] – sign – [rastro] – track – [pista] – clue

Follow-up

As a productive follow-up, all groups try to create a dialogue using as many of the words as possible from the winning maze.

Note

This activity, which was first suggested to me by Scott Thornbury, is fun and it alerts students to the potential for mistranslations when using bilingual and handheld dictionaries.

8.2 Production dictionaries

Aim	To introduce students to bilingual production dictionaries
Focus	Building vocabulary (in this lesson the focus is on character adjectives)
Level	Intermediate and above
Time	45 minutes
Preparation	You will need bilingual production dictionaries and a dice. Either write a short text focusing on vocabulary areas that you want to work on or use the description below or the one in activity 5.10. Check the dictionary that you are using for the keywords (in bold).

Procedure

1 Explain to the students that a bilingual production dictionary is like a very powerful bilingual thesaurus. You look up a common base word like *look* and find alternative words such as *examine, glimpse, glance, peer, scan* and *stare*, with definitions so that the meaning (and how the words differ in meaning) is clear. These dictionaries help broaden vocabulary and make writing and speaking more precise and expressive.

2 Tell them that in this activity, they will be improving this description of a famous person:

Scandal! _____ (a famous person) is not as nice as you might think! Most people think he/she is generous and kind, but actually he/she is **selfish, cruel** and _____!

3   Put the students into groups of four to six. Ask each group to appoint a scribe. Tell students that they are going to make numbered lists and you will throw the dice. Tell them to make only one list (per group) at a time. These are the instructions:

- First, make a list of six different **famous people**. Number them. *(At this point, you throw the dice. If, for example, a 4 comes up, the person at number 4 on each list is the person that group's story is going to be about.)*
- Now use the dictionary to make a list of six different words for *selfish*. Number them. *(When students have a list of six words, throw the dice.)*
- Now use the dictionary to make a list of six different words for *cruel*. Number them. *(You throw the dice.)*
- Finally, ask each group to think of another adjective for their famous person and use the dictionary to make a list of six different words for that adjective. *(When they are ready, throw the dice.)*

4   Give students time to go through their stories and check the spelling of the new words, adding any details they would like to make their stories more fun and interesting. Then ask them to read out their 'scandals'.

Variation

If your students like to read horoscopes, give them a bland description of a star sign to rewrite in more colourful language.

Picture dictionaries

There are some excellent new picture and photo dictionaries, for both young learners and adults.

In addition to the activities in chapter 6 (6.1 Picture this! Memory game and 6.7 Describe and draw), which can be used both with young learners and with adults, here are two more especially for young learners.

8.3 Memory game

Aim	To practise using the dictionary to learn new words
Focus	Vocabulary building
Level	Any
Age	Young learners (7–10 years)
Time	10–15 minutes
Preparation	Choose a rich (preferably double-page) spread in the picture dictionary.

Procedure

1 Ask students to work in groups or pairs. Tell them that they are going to get a chance to use their memories.
2 If you have multiple copies of the dictionary, ask each group to open their dictionaries to the pages you have selected. Alternatively, show the pages to the students.
3 Ask them to work together to try and remember as many words as possible in two to three minutes. (You can either allow them to write them down, or not, depending on their level and/or age.)
4 The group that remembers the most words wins.

Follow-up
Follow this up with a whole class chain story (one student says the first sentence of a story that uses at least one word from the activity, then another takes it over and the story continues until they have used all the words they can), or each group writes a separate story.

8.4 Picture snakes

Aim	To practise learning and writing new words
Focus	Topic vocabulary (the sample material practises the names of animals)
Age	Young learners (7–10 years)
Time	20–30 minutes
Preparation	Choose topic-based pictures (animals, food, games, etc.) for students to work on and one to use to introduce the activity.

Procedure

1 Show students the spread you have chosen. Elicit the words pictured. Write them on the board as students provide them.

```
ant bat bear camel dolphin elephant
fox giraffe gorilla hippopotamus
kangaroo lion lizard octopus rhinoceros
shark snake tiger tortoise wolf
```

2 Ask students to work in pairs and to write a word snake, using the last letter of a word to start the next word. Tell them to make the snake as long as they can, as quickly as they can.

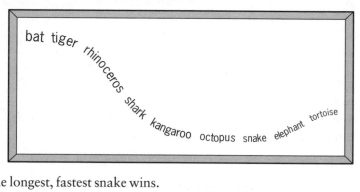

3 The longest, fastest snake wins.
4 Give pairs or groups different topic-based pages from the same picture dictionary to work from. They create word snakes to swap with another pair or group.

Phrasal verb dictionaries

Phrasal verb dictionaries are organized by the alphabetical order of the verb. Some verbs, like *get*, take a lot of particles, which can result in huge entries. Some of the phrasal verbs may have several meanings, so most phrasal verb dictionaries have guidewords, signposts or menus to help students find the right sense of the verb.

8.5 Phrasal verb + noun shuffle

Aim	To practise using the dictionary to find collocates
Focus	Phrasal verbs + nouns as objects/subjects
Level	Intermediate and above
Time	10–20 minutes
Preparation	Choose a group of phrasal verbs you have recently presented. Prepare cards like the ones below.

Procedure

1 Ask students to work in pairs and decide which groups of nouns go with which verbs, then check using their dictionaries.
2 Monitor and check.
3 Ask students to write a short story using each of the verbs with one of its collocates.
4 Ask students to swap stories, read them aloud, and then vote on their favourites.

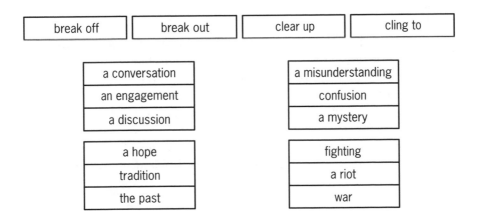

break off	break out	clear up	cling to

a conversation	a misunderstanding
an engagement	confusion
a discussion	a mystery

a hope	fighting
tradition	a riot
the past	war

Note

Some phrasal verb dictionaries, such as *Macmillan Phrasal Verbs Plus*, which the sample material is taken from, give collocate information explicitly in boxes. In other dictionaries, students will need to use the example sentences to do the activity.

Answers

break off – a conversation, an engagement, a discussion

fighting, a riot, war – *break out* (*breaks out* / *broke out*)

clear up – a misunderstanding, confusion, a mystery

cling to – a hope, tradition, the past

8.6 Pelmanism

Aim	To practise and/or revise phrasal verbs by topic
Focus	Phrasal verbs in topic areas
Level	Intermediate and above
Time	10–20 minutes
Preparation	Prepare sets of cards and answers like the ones in Box 56 in a topic area you want to practise or revise, or use the online version of the game (see Note 2 on page 142).

Procedure

1 Students work in groups of three: two play the game, the third checks their answers.

2 Place the cards face down on the table. The first player turns over three cards trying to get verb + particle + meaning cards that form a correct set.

3 If they don't, they turn the cards face down again and it is the other player's turn.

If a correct set is turned over, the player keeps the cards. The third student is the judge/referee.

4 Now give each group a topic and ask them to use their dictionaries to make cards (and answers) like these for the other students to play.

Box 56

✂

hack	into	to get into someone's computer system without their permission
log	off	to finish using a computer system
back	up	to make a copy of computer information so that you don't lose it
boot	up	to start up a computer so that it is ready for use

Answers

hack	into	to get into someone's computer system without their permission
log	off	to finish using a computer system
back	up	to make a copy of computer information so that you don't lose it
boot	up	to start up a computer so that it is ready for use

© Cambridge University Press 2007

Notes

1 This activity can also be done in a monolingual classroom with the card set made up of phrasal verb, definition and translation, for example:

do up	renovate	reformar

2 This is a 'manual' version of the Phrasal Verb Dispenser on the Cambridge Dictionaries website (www.dictionary.cambridge.org). If you can use the Phrasal Verb Dispenser online, then the checking is automatic and students can play alone, in pairs or groups of three before working on their own cards and answers.

The topics on the Cambridge site are: Computers (the sample material here), Conversation, Crime, Emotions, Food and drink, Illness, Money, Travel, Conversation.

Idioms dictionaries

Idioms dictionaries are great, and usually very popular with students once they have learned how to use them. Most idioms dictionaries are alphabetized by the first content word or keyword (noun or verb) rather than the first word of the idiom. Activity 8.7, which practises identifying keywords, is a good one to start with.

8.7 Keywords in idioms

Aim	To practise finding idioms quickly
Focus	Content words for entries
Level	Intermediate and above
Time	15–20 minutes
Preparation	Prepare a text which includes a number of idioms from a topic area you are working on or use the text in Box 57 (from the *Cambridge International Dictionary of Idioms* theme panels.) Replace the idioms with gaps. Good sources for idiom-rich texts are astrology websites, advertisements, songs, etc.

Procedure

1 Ask students to work in pairs or small groups. Give them the text and the idioms.
2 Ask them to underline the first keyword in the idiom and use their dictionaries to check whether they were correct.
3 Then put the correct idioms in the gaps.
4 Check as a whole class activity.

Box 57

Put the correct idioms in the gaps.

below par
did me a power of good
feeling a bit off colour
feeling like death warmed up
recharge my batteries
as right as rain
as white as a sheet

I'd been _____ for a while. I'd been more tired than usual and getting lots of headaches, and was generally a bit _____ . It was worst in the morning. I'd get up _____ . My mother commented that I was _____ . She suggested that I take a break and _____ . A week away from the office _____ . I came back feeling _____ .

© Cambridge University Press 2007

Answers (Box 57)

I'd been *feeling a bit off colour* for a while. I'd been more tired than usual and getting lots of headaches, and was generally a bit *below par*. It was worst in the morning. I'd get up *feeling like death warmed up*. My mother commented that I was *as white as a sheet*. She suggested that I take a break and *recharge my batteries*. A week away from the office *did me a power of good*. I came back feeling *as right as rain*.

8.8 Idioms in the media

Aim	To consolidate idiomatic vocabulary
Focus	Idioms in the media
Level	Intermediate and above
Time	15–20 minutes
Preparation	Find a headline that contains an idiom the students are likely to be familiar with. Also prepare a set of newspapers and magazines or, if you have access to the Internet, locate a few news or headlines sites.

Procedure

1 Put a recent headline on the board which contains an idiom which students might recognize. For example:

Italy strike gold as Zidane sees red

Ask students to write down the meaning of the headline, and then use their dictionaries (either online or print) to check whether they have understood it correctly.

2 Ask students to work in groups. Give them the newspapers, magazines or URLs of websites.

3 Ask each group to find as many idioms as they can (in headlines or advertisements) and use their dictionaries to check the meaning. Ask them to write their idioms on the board or an OHT and explain what the idioms mean and what the headline, article or advertisement is about.

4 Choose a local event and ask students to write a headline (that contains an idiom) for the story. Make it a competition – ask students to vote for their favourite headline.

Here are a few more headlines:
Half of Scottish farms in the red
Blue ribbon panel stumbles at finish line
Shuttle gets green light to fly home

Resources

Dictionaries

Pre-intermediate
Cambridge Essential Dictionary
Longman Wordwise
Oxford Essential Dictionary

Intermediate – Upper-intermediate
Cambridge Learner's Dictionary
Cambridge Dictionary of American English
Cambridge International Dictionary of Phrasal Verbs (English – French)
Cambridge International Dictionary of Idioms
Cambridge Dictionary of American Idioms

Longman Active Study Dictionary
Longman Essential Activator™

Macmillan Essential Dictionary
Macmillan Phrasal Verbs Plus

Oxford Learner's Dictionary
Oxford Wordfinder

Advanced
Cambridge Advanced Learner's Dictionary

Longman Dictionary of Contemporary English
Longman Language Activator™

Macmillan English Dictionary

Oxford Advanced Learner's Dictionary

Online learner dictionaries

These are dictionaries that you access on the Internet. The sites link to a server that holds the databases.

Cambridge Learner's Dictionary
Cambridge Advanced Learner's Dictionary
www.dictionary.cambridge.org

Macmillan English Dictionary
Macmillan Essential Dictionary
www.macmillandictionary.com

Simple English Wiktionary (from Wikipedia)
www.simple.wiktionary.org/wiki/Main_Page

Online etymology dictionaries

Online Etymology Dictionary
www.etymonline.com

Library Spot
A rich site with links to several reference sites
www.libraryspot.com/dictionaries/etymologydictionaries.htm

Concordancers and corpora

Virtual Language Centre
Teachers' toolbox, concordancer, text to voice, academic English
www.vlc.polyu.edu.hk/

The Compleat Lexical Tutor
Concordancer and corpora (and much, much more)
www.lextutor.ca/concordancers/

MICASE
Michigan Corpus of Academic Spoken English – searchable collection of transcripts of academic speech events
www.micase.umdl.umich.edu/m/micase/browse.html

Other useful websites

Academic Word List Software Site – Nottingham University
A very good site for students and teachers with free software to create
gapped or highlighted text using the Academic Word List
www.nottingham.ac.uk/~alzsh3/acvocab/

WordReference.com
English, French and Spanish definitions and translations as well as language
discussion forums
www.wordreference.com/

Wordsmyth
Crossword puzzle helper, anagram solver, vocabulary quiz builder and
glossary maker
www.wordsmyth.net/

Many things
Dictionary games based on topic word lists, linked to various dictionaries
www.manythings.org

English–Spanish online photo dictionary
www.my-spanish-dictionary.com

Index

NOTE: References in brackets and **bold** type refer to Activities.